GEOLOGY ENCYCLOPEDIAS

THE CRYSTAL AND GEMSTONE ENCYCLOPEDIA

BY SAMANTHA S. BELL

Encyclopedias

An Imprint of Abdo Reference
abdobooks.com

TABLE OF CONTENTS

EARTH'S TREASURES

Crystals and gemstones are Earth's treasures. Crystals form when atoms arrange into neat, repeating patterns. Atoms are tiny particles that make up all matter. They are categorized into elements, such as gold or carbon. Some crystals are made of only one element. Other crystals are compounds, made of multiple elements. Crystals, rocks, and organic materials that are recognized for their strength and beauty are called gemstones.

Most crystals and gemstones form below Earth's surface. When they are taken out of the ground, crystals are often rough and dull. Experts called lapidaries can cut and polish the raw materials into beautiful stones. Lapidaries often cut flat sides called facets into gemstones. Facets can bend and separate beams of light, showing different colors or effects.

Experts use a tool called the Mohs scale to measure the hardness of gemstones from 1 to 10. A gem's score reflects its ability to resist being scratched by other gemstones. A gemstone that ranks high on the Mohs scale can scratch one that ranks lower.

Some crystals naturally grow facets. These crystals may still be cut and polished to create different shapes.

Diamond is the only gemstone that ranks 10 on the Mohs scale.

Gemstones can be expensive. Their price is based on what are known as the four Cs. Some of the cost comes from the lapidary's work. This is called the cut. The other factors are natural. The second C is the color of the gem. The third C is clarity. Gemstones may have tiny cracks or other flaws that reduce their clarity, making them less valuable. The fourth C is carat, which measures the weight of the stone. One carat is equal to 0.007 ounces (0.2 g). Raw crystals are measured by similar characteristics.

Another reason gemstones and crystals can be expensive is that they can be rare. Some types are commonly found all over the world. But others are found in only one place on Earth and in limited quantities.

HOW CRYSTALS AND GEMSTONES FORM

Several natural processes can create the repeating pattern of atoms found in crystals. One process begins when water close to Earth's surface soaks into rocks and dissolves the minerals there. The minerals break up into many molecules suspended in the water. Molecules are groups of bonded atoms. As the water moves, it cools or evaporates. The molecules precipitate. This means they are no longer dissolved in water. They begin to bond with one another to form new materials.

Fluorite forms by precipitating from water containing the elements calcium and fluorine. Its symmetrical crystal structure means that fluorite often grows in cube-like shapes.

The type of crystal that forms depends on the elements that were dissolved. For example, rainwater flows through rocks on Earth's surface. It dissolves minerals containing sodium and chlorine atoms. This water flows into the ocean. When ocean water evaporates, the sodium and chlorine atoms bond. They form a crystal called sodium chloride, also known as table salt. This is a common crystal and not one that forms gemstones. But the same process works for many minerals.

MAGMA

Magma is hot, melted rock deep beneath Earth's surface. When it cools, crystals can grow inside magma. Gems that come from magma are created with lots of heat and pressure. These conditions are necessary for certain crystal structures to form. Heat and pressure affect the way atoms bond.

For example, diamond is made of carbon. Carbon can form several types of crystals. Carbon atoms arrange into the pattern

Crystals that form from magma are often found in places with volcanoes. Volcanoes are common where plates of Earth's crust move against one another.

that creates diamond only under high heat and pressure, such as in magma deep underground.

OTHER CONDITIONS

Heat and pressure are not the only conditions that influence how, where, and whether crystals grow. Crystals also need space. Water or magma may flow into open spaces, such as cracks in rocks. Crystals can form in the cracks. Crystal-filled cracks are known as veins.

Crystals also need time to grow. The speed at which they grow depends on the dissolved minerals, the substance in which they are dissolved, and the way they form. Some crystals can grow in just a few hours or days. Others take thousands or even millions of years.

Sometimes the pattern of atoms in a crystal is not perfect. Another substance may be present. This is called an inclusion. Inclusions can be trace elements or small amounts of trapped gas or liquid. Inclusions give some gemstones their beautiful characteristics.

DIGGING UP THE TREASURE

Once crystals and gemstones form underground, they may come to the surface. People mine some gemstones by digging

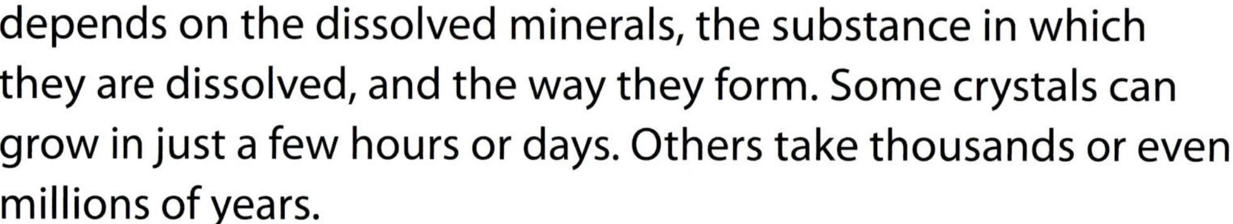

Rutile is a mineral that can form long, thin inclusions in quartz and tourmaline gemstones.

for them. Other gems are brought to the surface through natural processes. Magma can carry gems up during a volcanic eruption. Sometimes Earth's surface cracks or moves, causing rocks to shift, bend, or break. This can push rocks from deep underground closer to the surface.

After rocks come to the surface, the gems inside them can be released in several ways. Wind, rain, ice, and other natural forces slowly break down some rocks over time. This is called weathering, or erosion. Some minerals dissolve and disappear. But crystals and gems may be released from rocks and carried away by rainwater. As the water flows, it moves the gems. People might find them in streams, along ocean shorelines, or in sand.

GEOLOGIC TIMESCALE

Earth formed more than 4.5 billion years ago. To better understand this huge stretch of time, scientists use the geologic timescale. This timeline is divided into eons, eras, periods, and epochs. By studying crystal and gemstone formations, scientists can better understand how conditions on Earth changed over time.

The Precambrian Era is a stretch of time that includes three eons. It lasted from about 4.5 billion to 541 million years ago. During this time, gemstones including diamonds and zircons formed deep in Earth. They were later brought to the surface through volcanic eruptions.

During the Paleozoic Era, many gemstones formed deep in Earth's crust. Crystals slowly grew in underground openings. Across millions of years, erosion brought these crystals to the surface. The Mesozoic Era was the age of dinosaurs. Amber formed during this time, preserving some fossils.

The Cenozoic Era began 66 million years ago. It stretches through the modern day. During this period, many gemstones have formed near Earth's surface. They develop in cracks in rocks. Other gemstones form as volcanoes erupt with lava. Natural processes continue to create crystals and gemstones today.

Sapphire likely formed in Earth about 150 million years ago, during the Mesozoic Era.

EON	ERA	PERIOD	EPOCH	MYA*
Phanerozoic	Cenozoic	Quaternary	Holocene	0.01
			Pleistocene	2.6
		Neogene	Pliocene	5.3
			Miocene	23.0
		Paleogene	Oligocene	33.9
			Eocene	56.0
			Paleocene	66.0
	Mesozoic	Cretaceous		145.0
		Jurassic		201.3
		Triassic		251.9
	Paleozoic	Permian		298.9
		Pennsylvanian		323.2
		Mississippian		358.9
		Devonian		419.2
		Silurian		443.8
		Ordovician		485.4
		Cambrian		541.0
Proterozoic Archean Hadean	Precambrian			2500
				4000
				4600

*Million Years Ago

Blue lace agate is a variety that includes pale blue and white bands.

AGATE

Agate is a gemstone known for its colorful, layered appearance. It is a type of quartz, which is one of the most plentiful minerals in Earth's crust. Agate can form in several kinds of rocks. It forms most often in volcanic rocks, or rocks made by volcanoes.

Agate is made up of layers called bands that form over time. These bands can be white, gray, yellowish brown, or reddish brown. They can also be blue or green. The colors are caused mainly by tiny crystals of iron and manganese oxide in the soil. Sometimes minerals besides iron and manganese oxide mix in with the agate. This can change the color of certain layers.

BANDS ON DISPLAY

Agate gets its name from the Achates River in Sicily, the Italian island where it was first discovered. Today the river is called the Dirillo. People can find agates all over the world. Places where these gems are most common include Brazil, Mexico, the United States, Namibia, India, and Scotland.

Most agates are about the size of peas. But they can be as big as bowling balls. Many jewelry designers use the gemstones' natural patterns to create unique pieces. Agates are also used for carvings and beads.

Larger agates are often cut into thin slices to show their colorful bands.

FINDING AGATE

- Agate can be found around the world.
- Most agate forms in volcanic rock. Over time, the rock surrounding agate erodes. The crystal is left behind.
- After the agate is exposed, it may break off and wash away. Some of the best places to find agates include beaches, rivers, and dry riverbeds.
- Agate is more common in areas where there are volcanoes.
- Agate crystals can be cut and polished for use as gemstones.

Bands of agate form over the course of millions of years.

Many agates sold today have been dyed to show brighter colors.
Inclusions give some bands of agate their color.
Some layers of agate are made of the same material but have different crystal structures.

ALEXANDRITE

Alexandrite is a rare gemstone formed from the mineral chrysoberyl. Its color changes depending on the light. In daylight, it looks bluish green. Under lamplight or candlelight, it looks purplish red. This effect happens because there is a tiny amount of an element called chromium inside the gem. Chromium changes the crystal structure in a way that makes the

Because of its color-changing effect, alexandrite is sometimes said to be emerald by day, ruby by night.

gem reflect different colors of light. It is the same element that gives emeralds their green color.

It takes just the right elements and conditions for alexandrite to form. Along with chromium, alexandrite is also made of beryllium. These elements must come together in metamorphic rocks deep underground.

ROYAL NAMESAKE

Alexandrite was discovered in 1830 in the Ural Mountains in Russia. It was named after Prince Alexander II. Its red and green colors matched the national military colors of Russia at the time. Today most alexandrite comes from eastern Africa, Sri Lanka, and Brazil.

RATING CRYSTALS AND GEMSTONES ON THE MOHS SCALE

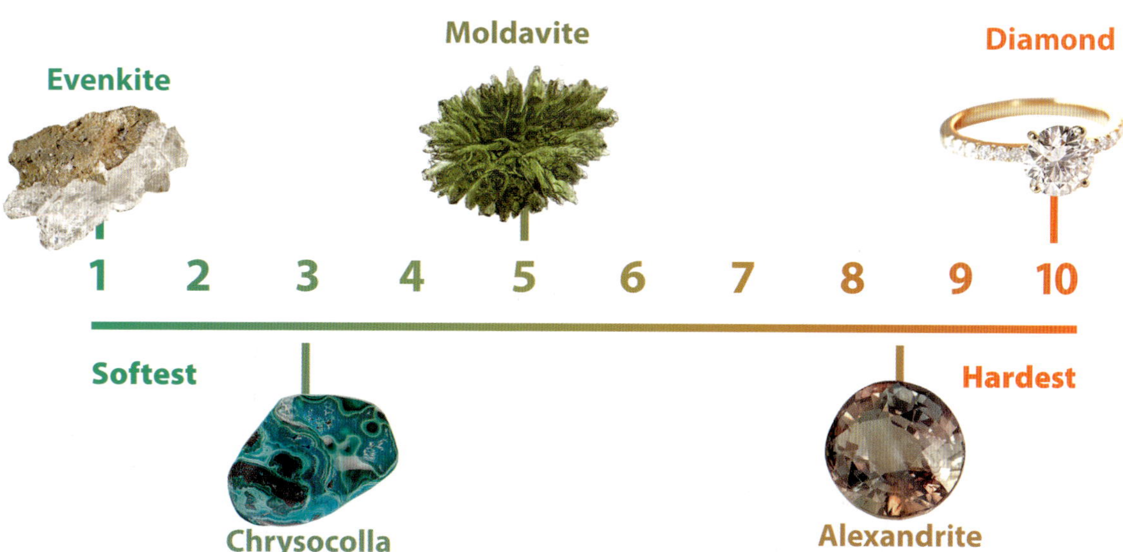

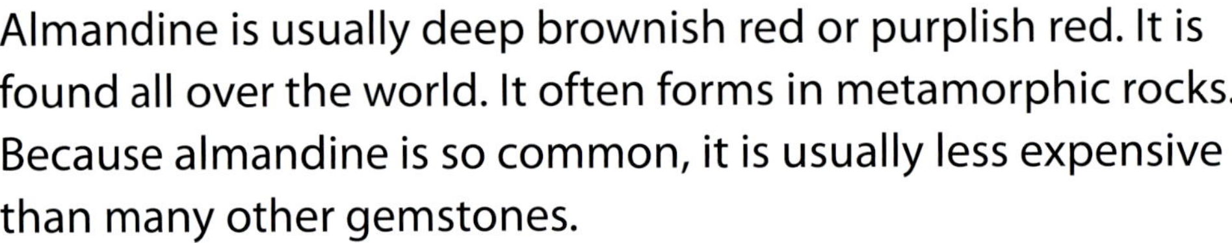

Almandine gets its color from elements including iron, manganese, and magnesium.

ALMANDINE

Almandine is the most common type of garnet. Garnet is a group of gemstones that come in almost every color. Almandine is usually deep brownish red or purplish red. It is found all over the world. It often forms in metamorphic rocks. Because almandine is so common, it is usually less expensive than many other gemstones.

FIRE-LIKE GLOW

Ancient Egyptians used almandines in jewelry as early as 3500 BCE. In the 70s CE, Roman scholar Pliny the Elder called the brightest red gems *carbunculus*, meaning they looked like they were on fire. This group included almandine. Georgius Agricola gave the gem its current name in 1546. He named it after the ancient city Alabanda in modern-day Turkey. Alabanda was an ancient gem-cutting center. This may have been where almandine was cut into gemstones.

Almandine has a hardness of 7 to 7.5 on the Mohs scale. This makes it strong enough for most types of jewelry. Besides being used as a gemstone, almandine is also useful as an abrasive. It is added to grinding wheels, saws, and sandpaper to make their surfaces rough.

Almandine often forms in a type of rock called schist. Schist provides a structure for crystals to grow. When the rock is washed away, the crystals remain.

Amazonite is often cut into a rounded shape rather than a faceted one. Since this gem is not transparent, facets would not cause the same light-bending effects that they do in clearer stones.

AMAZONITE

Amazonite is a gemstone that forms from the mineral feldspar. Its color can range from light green to bluish green. The green color likely comes from tiny amounts of lead in the stone. Amazonite was named after the Amazon River in South America, where some similar green gemstones were found. However, amazonite has never been found near the river.

ANCIENT ART

People have been making beads and carvings from amazonite for thousands of years. As far back as 5200 BCE, people in northern Africa, Mesopotamia, and the Indus River Valley were working with amazonite. The ancient Egyptians believed the stone gave people courage. They used it in jewelry and decorations. Some cultures believed it could help calm or comfort people.

Amazonite has been found in Russia, Madagascar, Brazil, and Ethiopia. Some of the best amazonite comes from Pikes Peak in Colorado. Amazonite has a hardness of 6 to 6.5 on the Mohs scale. It can be easily scratched. But it is still a good jewelry stone for earrings and necklaces. It is also used to make beads and decorative objects.

AMBER

Amber is an organic gem. It comes from living organisms. Amber forms when sticky sap from certain trees hardens. Only two types of trees living today produce resin that can form amber, and the process takes tens of thousands to millions of years. Most amber is from ancient trees.

Yellow, orange, and brown are the most common colors of amber. Sometimes amber contains a tiny animal or part of a plant. These organisms became trapped in the sap as it hardened.

DID YOU KNOW?

Amber is one of the few ways that small, fragile organisms can be successfully preserved. These delicate fossils provide important information about ancient plants and animals.

Insects are common organisms to be fossilized in amber.

GEM OF THE PAST

Amber can be clear or cloudy. The cloudy appearance is usually caused by tiny gas bubbles trapped as the sap turned to amber. Clear amber is used for fine jewelry. Cloudier pieces may be made into objects such as cups, bowls, and umbrella handles.

Some types of amber are found in the ground. Others have been carried by the ocean. The Baltic coastline in Germany, Poland, and Russia is an important source of amber.

AMETHYST

Amethyst is a type of quartz. It comes in many shades of purple, from soft lilac to deep reddish purple. Some amethysts are so light that the color is difficult to see. Others are so dark they are difficult to see through.

The color can also vary within the same crystal. This uneven coloring is called color zoning. Color zoning occurs when different amounts of iron enter the crystal as it grows. Most people want an amethyst with strong and even color.

FEBRUARY'S GEM

Amethyst has a hardness of 7 on the Mohs scale. It is strong enough to use in any type of jewelry, including rings, bracelets,

Amethyst receives its color from the presence of iron and other trace elements.

and earrings. People also use amethysts to create carvings, beads, and other decorative objects. Amethysts used to be as expensive as rubies and emeralds. But in the 1800s, miners discovered large deposits of amethyst in Brazil. This abundance lowered the price of the gem. Today the major sources of amethyst are Brazil and Uruguay. Amethyst is the birthstone for February.

CELEBRATING WITH STONES

In modern tradition, every month of the year is represented by one to three gemstones known as birthstones. Historians believe the use of birthstones goes back to ancient times. The first official list was created in 1912 by the Jewelers of America. Gifting a birthstone based on someone's birth month has become a popular tradition. Jewelry using a birthstone may also represent a loved one born in that month.

AMETRINE

Ametrine is a gemstone that naturally combines two types of quartz. It is part amethyst and part citrine. Amethyst is purple, and citrine is golden yellow to orange. Ametrine shows both purple and yellow bands. The purple and yellow colors in each gem blend together in unique ways.

LOST AND FOUND

Most of the world's ametrine comes from the Anahí mine in Bolivia. Legend says that a Spanish explorer discovered the mine's location in the 1600s. He was given the mine when he married a local princess named Anahí. After that, the mine was forgotten for more than 300 years. It was finally rediscovered in the 1960s. The mine was named Anahí after the legendary princess.

Ametrine has a hardness of 7 on the Mohs scale. It makes a beautiful jewelry stone. Some lapidaries create unusual cuts to showcase the stone's unique color combination.

Some ametrine stones are bright and show a clear line between the two colors. Those are considered the most valuable.

The colors of ametrine may appear more mixed in its rough form. Lapidaries can emphasize the division between its colors while cutting gemstones.

AMMOLITE

Ammolite is an organic gemstone. It comes from fossilized shells of extinct sea creatures called ammonites. These ocean-dwelling mollusks lived between 388 and 66 million years ago. The creatures' shells were made of the mineral aragonite. Under very specific temperature and pressure conditions, aragonite forms a gemstone.

Ammolite is known for its iridescence. That means it reflects light so that it appears to shimmer with different colors when looked at from various angles. The highest-quality ammolite is bright and shows a full range of colors.

CANADA'S TREASURE

Ammonite fossils can be found all over the world. But the ammolite gemstone can be found only in the Bearpaw Formation in Alberta, Canada. The Bearpaw Formation is a geologic formation that contains fossils from many prehistoric creatures, including dinosaurs.

The exact appearance of ammolite depends on the pressure and temperature it experienced during formation.

Ammonite fossils covered with ammolite are especially valuable.

Ammolite is one of the world's rarest and most valuable gemstones. The quality of ammolite is based on the gemstone's brilliance and variety of color. Certain colors, such as crimson, violet, and gold, are very rare and in high demand. Ammolite has a hardness of 3.5 to 4 on the Mohs scale.

Uncut andalusite displays a variety of colors. In faceted gemstones, the colors appear one at a time or blended together.

ANDALUSITE

Andalusite is a mineral found in aluminum-rich rocks. It forms under low pressure. Although it can be used as a gemstone, andalusite is better known for forming rocks. Andalusite often appears in metamorphic rocks, where it forms columns of pink crystals.

Andalusite displays a trait called pleochroism. This means it can show different colors from different angles. Some stones can even display three colors at the same time. The colors may be pink, red, pale brown, green, yellow, or white.

NAMING MIX-UP

Andalusite gets its name from the Spanish region of Andalusia. Some of the earliest of these gemstones were collected there in the late 1700s. For a long time, people believed this was where the crystal was first discovered. The actual discovery location was El Cardoso de la Sierra, another location in Spain. But the original name stuck.

Andalusite has a hardness of 6.5 to 7.5 on the Mohs scale. Although it is strong enough for jewelry, it is not well known or commonly used. Today Brazil is the main source of gem-quality andalusite. Other sources include the United States, Belgium, Myanmar, Sri Lanka, and Australia.

Chiastolite is a type of andalusite noted for a cross-shaped inclusion of graphite in the stone.

Polished apatite can be used to create beads for jewelry.

APATITE

Apatite is the name for a group of gemstones. Several gemstones, such as fluorapatite, mimetite, and moroxite, belong to this group. However, they are usually just called apatite. Apatite forms from minerals that contain the element phosphorus.

Apatite crystals come in various colors. The most common are greens and blues. Apatite can also be yellow, purple, pink, brown, or clear. Due to their structure, some apatite crystals can glow under special lights called ultraviolet (UV) lights. This trait is called fluorescence.

MORE THAN JEWELRY

For many years, no one knew much about apatite. But in the late 1900s, miners discovered neon bluish-green apatite in Madagascar. Since then, more people have used apatite of all colors in jewelry. People create most of the bright blue apatite seen today by heating naturally green stones.

Apatite can be found throughout the world. The major sources for gem-quality apatite are Brazil, Myanmar, and Mexico. Apatite has a hardness of 5 on the Mohs scale. This means it needs to be treated carefully if used in jewelry.

The mineral apatite is the main natural source of the element phosphorus. This element is one of the primary ingredients used in fertilizer for plants.

AQUAMARINE

Aquamarine is one of several gemstones that come from a mineral called beryl. The gemstone that forms from beryl depends on tiny amounts of other elements that are included when the crystal forms. The color of aquamarine comes from iron. This color ranges from very light blue to dark bluish or blue green. Larger stones are usually richer in color. Darker stones are very valuable.

TIED TO THE SEA

The name *aquamarine* comes from the Latin words meaning "water" and "sea." The gem has been linked to seas throughout history. For example, Roman fishermen believed it brought them luck in catching fish and protection for safe travel by boat.

Aquamarine is found in many countries. However, it is mined mostly in Brazil. Some stones grow to be very large, reaching 1 foot (0.3 m) in length. Aquamarine is one of two birthstones for March.

Aquamarine crystals may form in several kinds of rocks. Uncut crystals often grow in a hexagonal shape.

Aquamarine has a hardness of 7.5 to 8 on the Mohs scale.
This makes it a good choice for jewelry, including rings.

Aragonite crystals may grow in interesting shapes when given space to do so.

ARAGONITE

Aragonite is a colorless, white, or gray crystal. It may also have hints of blue, green, red, or violet. Aragonite can be found in sedimentary rocks or caves. It is also found in the ocean. Many marine animals, including corals, snails, and clams, use the mineral form of aragonite to create their shells and hard parts.

Aragonite is made of calcium carbonate. This is the same compound that makes up the mineral calcite. However, calcium carbonate can form different patterns, creating two different crystals. Aragonite crystals are long and needle shaped. Calcite crystals are shorter and blockier.

COLLECTOR'S CHOICE

Aragonite was named in 1797 by Abraham Gottlob Werner. He named it for the village in Spain where it was discovered, Molina de Aragón. Aragonite measures 3.5 to 4 on the Mohs scale. Crystals that can be cut into gemstones are almost always very small. Because of this, faceted aragonite gems are collector's items.

Benitoite is fluorescent, shining bright blue under UV light.

BENITOITE

Benitoite is one of the rarest gemstones in the world. It is sometimes called the blue diamond because of its deep, transparent blue color. It can also be pink or colorless. Because of its beauty and rarity, benitoite can be expensive. Stones with a rich blue color cost more than stones that are very light or very dark.

CALIFORNIA'S GEM

Benitoite was first discovered in 1907. A gem hunter named James M. Couch found the crystals in the San Benito Mountains in California. At first, he thought they were sapphires. But a scientist named George Louderback used the Mohs hardness test to check them. He realized these crystals were something different because they were softer than sapphires. The new gemstone was named benitoite after the place where it had been found.

Benitoite has since been discovered in a few other places around the world. But no other place has produced gem-quality crystals. With a hardness of 6 to 6.5, benitoites can be used in most jewelry settings.

Benitoite is California's state gemstone.

BLOODSTONE

Bloodstone is a gemstone that comes in two different forms. One is called heliotrope. It is somewhat transparent and has red spots. The red spots are caused by a compound called iron oxide. The other type is called plasma. It is a solid dark green color and has few or no red spots.

LEGENDS AND LORE

Bloodstone gets its name from its red spots. These may look like drops of blood. Bloodstone has been part of many stories through history. In ancient times, people believed it would turn red in the setting Sun. Some people also believed bloodstone could help stop bleeding.

Bloodstones with many red spots usually sell for high prices.

Bloodstone is usually found in rocks or as pebbles in
riverbeds. It is found mainly in India, Brazil, and Australia. It is
one of two birthstones for March. Bloodstone has a hardness of
6.5 to 7 on the Mohs scale.

Imperfections are common in larger, faceted brazilianite gems.

BRAZILIANITE

Brazilianite is a gemstone that contains the compound phosphate. It is bright green to yellowish green in color. It forms deep underground in rocks made from cooled magma. It is often found with other minerals such as albite, muscovite, and quartz.

Brazilianite can show different colors when viewed from different angles. In natural light, it usually appears as a rich green color. But under artificial light, it may appear yellow or yellowish green. This trait is known as pleochroism.

NAMED FOR A COUNTRY

Brazilianite was discovered in Minas Gerais, Brazil, in 1944. It was named by Frederick Harvey Pough and Edward Porter Henderson in honor of the country. Brazil is still the major source of gem-quality brazilianite. But brazilianite can also be found in many other countries. Brazilianite rates a 5.5 to 6 on the Mohs scale.

Brazilianite crystals often form in the shape of rods or droplets.

CARNELIAN

Carnelian is part of the chalcedony family of quartz. Chalcedony stones are smooth and made of microscopic crystals. Carnelian's color ranges from orange and yellowish orange to reddish orange and reddish brown. Carnelian gets its color from iron in the stone.

DID YOU KNOW?

Some elements can cause many colors in gems. The effect of the element depends on the structure of a crystal. Iron can color gems blue, green, orange, yellow, brown, or black.

Carnelian becomes darker when heated, even when it is heated only by the Sun.

MYTHS AND MEANINGS

People all over the ancient world valued carnelian for its beauty. It was also easy to carve or cut into jewelry stones. Carnelian came to symbolize health, luck, and royalty. Among Arab peoples, it was considered one of the stones of kings. During the Middle Ages and Renaissance, some people believed carnelian could give a person courage, calm anger, or stop bad dreams.

Carnelian is found in many parts of the world. However, India has been the center for producing carnelian beads for centuries. Other countries that produce gem-quality stones include Brazil, Egypt, and Uruguay. Carnelian has a hardness of 6.5 to 7 on the Mohs scale.

The colorful, swirling effects of charoite are often invisible until the stone is polished.

CHAROITE

Charoite is a mineral that forms large crystals and can be cut into gemstones. The mineral is purple in color. Other mineral inclusions may be shades of white, gray, or brown. The crystals in charoite are packed tightly together. This creates the famous swirling patterns that make this mineral unique. Charoite forms deep in Earth's crust as rocks combine under high heat and intense pressure.

RARE DISCOVERY

Charoite was discovered in 1949. It was confirmed as a new mineral in 1977. Charoite was named after the Chara River in Siberia, Russia. It has been found in only this location. Charoite has a hardness that ranges from 5 to 6 on the Mohs scale. It should be protected if used in jewelry to keep it from being damaged. Charoite is also used to make decorative objects such as bookends and vases.

Due to its low Mohs rating, charoite is safer in necklaces and earrings than in rings, where it may be scratched more easily.

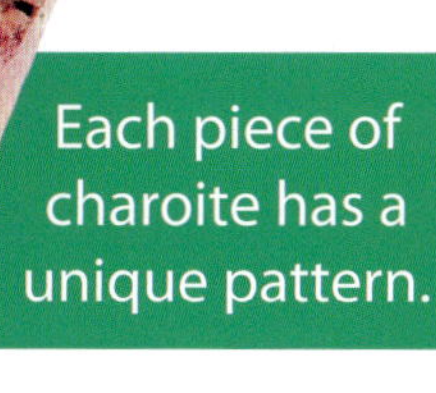

Each piece of charoite has a unique pattern.

CHICKEN-BLOOD STONE

Chicken-blood stone is a mixture of clay minerals and quartz. This material has several natural colors, which blend or combine in different layers. These include yellow, green, blue, purple, gray, black, and white. Chicken-blood stone also contains the bright red mineral cinnabar. This gives the stone its red color. The red may appear as spots or streaks.

Chicken-blood stones used as gems usually contain a lot of cinnabar. Some stones contain so much cinnabar that they are completely red. The most valuable stones are bright red. These are rare and prized by collectors.

DID YOU KNOW?

A chicken-blood stone should not be displayed in direct sunlight. Sunlight causes the cinnabar to turn dark red or even black.

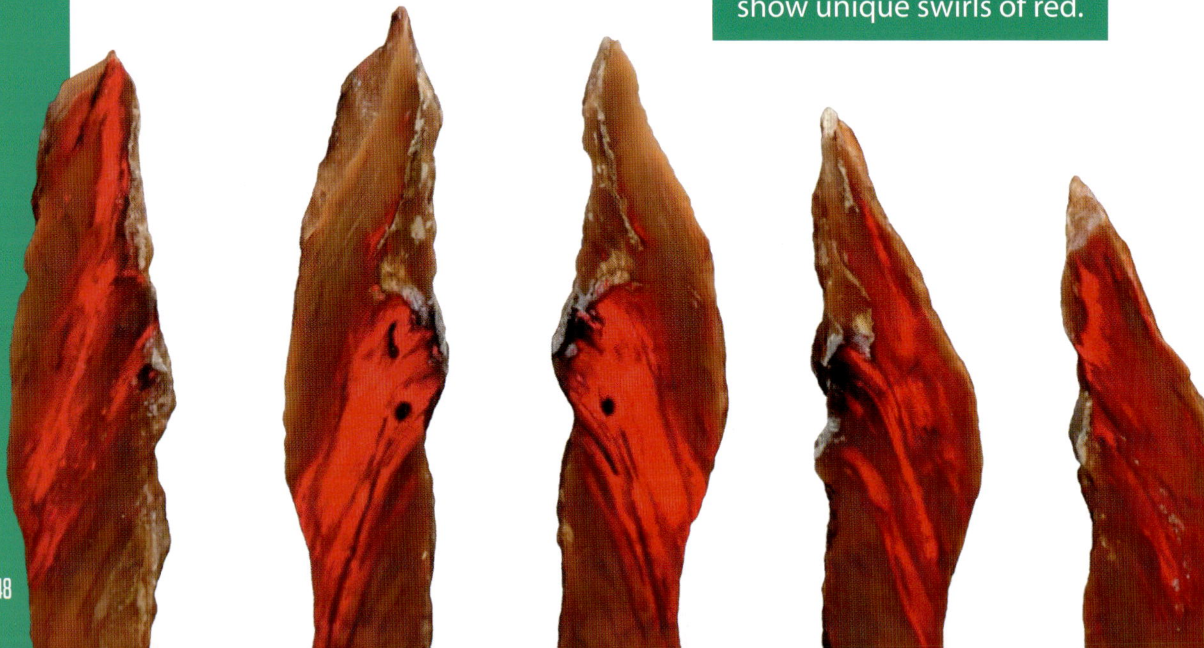

Chicken-blood stones show unique swirls of red.

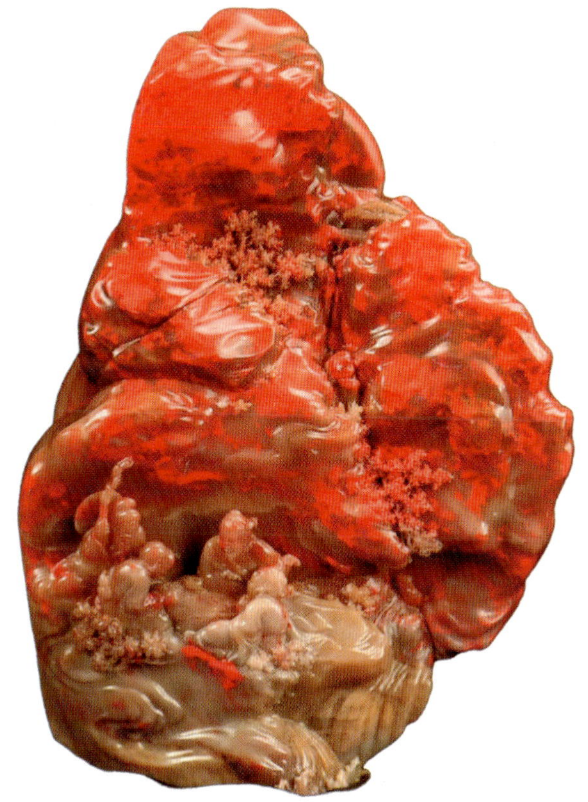

GOOD LUCK STONE

Chicken-blood stone is mined only in China. Its name comes from the red streaks. Local residents who first found the stone thought it looked like chicken blood. Red has symbolized good luck in Chinese culture since ancient times. For hundreds of years, the stone was used to create important seals and beautiful carvings. The material ranges from 6.5 to 7 on the Mohs scale.

Chrome diopside ranges in clarity. Some stones are transparent, while others are opaque.

CHROME DIOPSIDE

Chrome diopside is a brilliant green gemstone. Its rich color comes from an element called chromium. This is the same element that gives emerald its deep green color. However, chrome diopside is much more affordable than emerald. Chrome diopside can range from light green to a dark green that looks almost black. The color becomes darker as the gem gets bigger.

STONE OF PEACE

Mines began producing chrome diopside for sale in the 1980s. Throughout the gem's history, some people believed it brought peace. Others believed it helped loved ones who had died move on to a new life. In some cultures, people believed placing it on one's forehead at night brought sweet dreams.

Chrome diopside can be found around the world. But gem-quality chrome diopside can be found only in the Siberian tundra in Russia. That is one of the coldest places on Earth. Because of these conditions, chrome diopside can be mined only in the summer. It has a hardness of 5 to 6 on the Mohs scale.

Chrome diopside is also called the Russian emerald.

CHRYSOBERYL

Chrysoberyl is a very hard and durable mineral. It forms in metamorphic rocks that contain beryllium. Its color can range from honey gold to green to brown. There are several types of chrysoberyl. One of these is called cat's-eye. Stones of this type show a thin line that resembles a cat's pupil. Other gemstones have this effect. But in chrysoberyl, it is very strong. When the term *cat's-eye* is used alone, it always refers to chrysoberyl.

MISTAKEN MINERAL

For many years, scientists thought chrysoberyl was a type of beryl. Its name comes from the Greek word *chrysos*, meaning "gold," and the word *beryl*. But in the late 1700s, scientists learned it was a different mineral than beryl. Chrysoberyl has

Chrysoberyl has a hardness of 8.5 on the Mohs scale.

been prized by cultures for thousands of years. Some people
even viewed it as a good luck charm.

Chrysoberyl can be found in countries around the world.
Some of these include Brazil, Madagascar, Myanmar, Pakistan,
Russia, the United States, and Zimbabwe. The transparent
variety of chrysoberyl makes beautiful gemstones for jewelry.

CHRYSOCOLLA

Chrysocolla is a gemstone that develops in places rich in copper. It usually appears after other rocks and minerals have already formed. Chrysocolla can be found in different shapes. Some chrysocolla stones look like smooth, rounded clumps. Others have a bubbly crust that forms on the surface of rocks. Chrysocolla can appear green, bluish green, blue, black, or brown. Rare pieces may even be yellow.

Chrysocolla rarely forms as crystals, which leads to its unusual and organic shapes.

STRENGTHENED WITH SILICA

The Greek philosopher Theophrastus named chrysocolla in 315 BCE. The name comes from the Greek words *chrysos*, meaning "gold," and *kolla*, which means "glue." Long ago, people used chrysocolla to join together pieces of gold when making jewelry or tools.

Chrysocolla is a very soft gemstone. It measures just 2.5 to 3.5 on the Mohs scale. For this reason, it is often mixed with a mineral called silica. The silica makes it harder. Then it can be used as a jewelry stone. Chrysocolla without much silica will crumble when it is cut.

CINNABAR

Cinnabar is a mineral that contains the element mercury. This mineral's gemstones can be found in different shades of red, including bright red, violet red, and brownish red. Cinnabar can form in many ways. Its crystals are usually thick and flat. The crystals often have fine lines or grooves on them. They may appear in diamond or star shapes.

BEAUTIFUL BUT DANGEROUS

Cinnabar has been used by many civilizations throughout history. In China, it was used in medicine. People in Italy, Greece, Spain, Japan, China, Turkey, and South America used it as a pigment. It rates only 2 to 2.5 on the Mohs scale. Because it is so soft, it can be ground up into a very fine powder. When mixed with liquids, it has been used to make paint. Some people even used cinnabar in makeup. However, people later learned that the mercury in cinnabar is toxic. For this reason, it is no longer used in makeup.

Some cinnabar jewelry is still made. The stone may be covered in a layer of protective resin or lacquer to ensure the mercury in the stone does not harm the wearer.

CITRINE

Citrine is a variety of quartz. Natural citrine is very rare. It is usually pale yellow. The color is caused by iron in the gemstone.

Most citrine available today is created by heating smoky quartz or amethyst. The heat causes the stone to change color. Pale violet amethysts are often used. The color of the amethysts used can determine the richness of the citrines' yellow color. They may become yellow, orangish red, or orangish brown.

Citrine is often mistaken for yellow topaz, since the two gems are very similar in color.

HEALING STONES

Many people believe certain crystals have healing properties. They say that the stones can help them physically and emotionally. Even though there is no scientific proof, some people still use crystals for these benefits. For example, citrine is known as the stone of abundance. Some people think it can help bring more confidence and success.

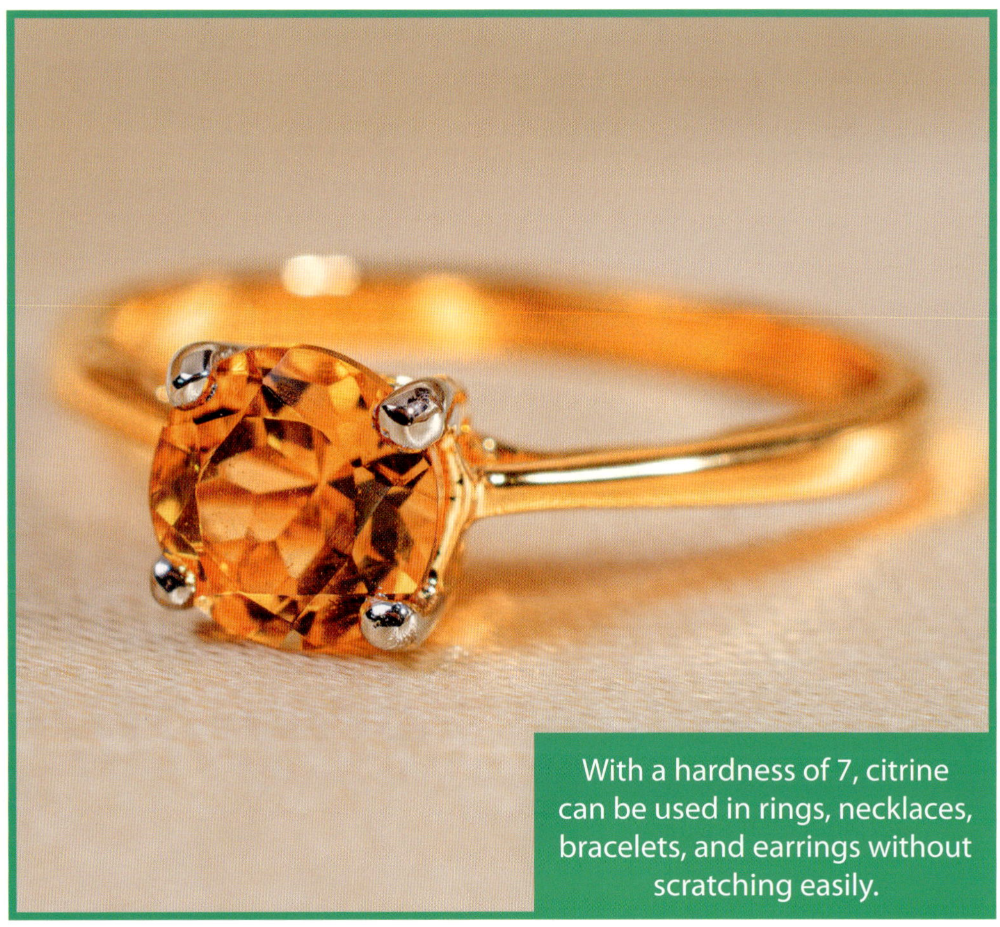

YELLOW FAVORITE

Citrine is one of the most popular yellow gemstones. It is also one of the birthstones for November. Citrine makes a good jewelry stone.

Almost all natural citrine comes from Brazil. Like most quartz, citrine is available in large sizes. This makes it a good stone for lapidaries to work with. They can easily form it into interesting shapes.

DANBURITE

Danburite is a gemstone known for its clarity and soft colors. It can be transparent like glass or a little cloudy. It often appears pale yellow, yellowish brown, or light pink. Some danburite has no color at all. Most danburite shows a sky-blue fluorescence under UV light.

LOST GEMS

Danburite is named after Danbury, Connecticut. It was first discovered there in 1839 by Charles Shepherd. Today the original deposit is buried under the city. Danburite is now found in many countries around the world. These include Mexico, the United States, Japan, Switzerland, and Madagascar.

Danburite is not a rare gemstone. But large crystals that can be cut into gem shapes are hard to find. Danburite has a hardness of 7 to 7.5 on the Mohs scale.

Some danburite is a bright lemon-yellow color.

DIAMOND

Diamonds are gemstones made of only one element: carbon. They are formed deep within Earth where it is very hot. There is also a lot of pressure from the rock above. The heat and pressure cause diamond crystals to grow. Diamonds have the highest luster, or shine, of any gemstone. They split light into a rainbow of colors.

Since the mid-1900s, diamonds have been the most popular stones used in engagement rings.

The Hope Diamond weighs 45.52 carats, or about 0.32 ounces (9.1 g).

JEWELRY AND TOOLS

People in ancient India, Greece, and Rome wrote about diamonds. The first recorded diamond mines were in India. By the 1720s, Brazil had become the largest diamond producer. In the 1860s, diamonds were discovered in South Africa. Today the top three diamond-producing countries are Botswana, Russia, and Canada.

Diamonds are the birthstone for April. But jewelry is not their only use. Diamonds are the hardest natural material on Earth, ranking 10 on the Mohs scale. Diamonds are so hard they can be scratched only by another diamond. Because diamonds are so hard, they are used in tools for cutting, grinding, drilling, and polishing.

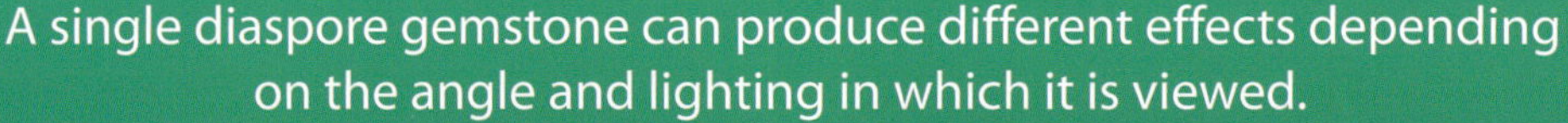
A single diaspore gemstone can produce different effects depending on the angle and lighting in which it is viewed.

DIASPORE

The gemstone diaspore comes from the mineral of the same name. Gem-quality diaspore is rare and often highly valued. Diaspore changes color under different lighting. It appears green or golden in daylight and shows pink or purple tones under indoor lighting. It can also show variations of peach, light brown, or soft yellow depending on the type and angle of light.

TURKISH TREASURE

The name *diaspore* comes from a Greek word that means "to scatter." This is because diaspore falls apart when tested with a blowpipe flame. A blowpipe flame is a small, focused flame used to test minerals by heating them.

People first discovered gem-quality diaspore in the 1980s. However, they did not start mining the gems to sell until the early 2000s. Diaspore can be found throughout the world. Some of the best gem-quality diaspore forms in the mountains of Turkey. These gemstones are also called by the brand names Zultanite and Csarite. The name *Zultanite* is based on the word *sultan*, a ruler in the ancient Turkish empire. *Csarite* is based on the word *czar*, a name for the ruler of Russia. Diaspore has a hardness on the Mohs scale of 6.5 to 7.

Diaspore fluoresces yellowish green under UV light.

EMERALD

Emerald is a gemstone that comes from the mineral beryl. It is known as one of the three precious gemstones, along with rubies and sapphires. Emeralds range from light green to deep, rich green. The deeper the color, the more valuable the stone is. Emeralds often have flaws and cracks. Most emeralds are treated with oils. The oils fill in cracks on the surface and improve the stone's clarity.

TREASURED BY MANY

Ancient Egyptians used emeralds in jewelry and burial practices. In South America, the Muzo people of Colombia had prized emerald mines. The Incas and Aztecs honored emerald in their religious rituals.

Emeralds are found all over the world, with 60 percent coming from Colombia. Emeralds measure 7.5 to 8 on the Mohs scale. However, because of their flaws, they can be damaged more easily than other stones of this hardness.

Many uncut emeralds can look cloudy due to inclusions.

NATURAL VS. LAB GROWN

Natural gemstones form beneath Earth's surface. Many of these stones take thousands of years to form. Because the conditions underground vary, each is unique. Lab-grown gemstones are created in a laboratory using advanced technology. These gems have the same properties as natural gemstones. But they are made in just weeks or months. They do not have any of the flaws found in natural gems. Lab-grown emeralds are more affordable than natural ones.

Euclase is often found in a type of rock called granite.

EUCLASE

Euclase is a gemstone formed from the metals beryllium and aluminum. It is best known for its beautiful blue crystals. These range from pale blue to navy blue. The slender crystals are shaped like prisms with noticeable grooves. Besides blue, euclase crystals may be pale green, deep yellowish green, greenish blue, pink, white, and violet. However, most crystals are colorless. Many of these are treated with radiation to turn them blue or green.

BRITTLE BEAUTY

The name *euclase* comes from the Greek words *eu* and *klasis*. Together these words mean "good fracture." This is because the crystals can be brittle. Euclase measures 6.5 to 7.5 on the Mohs scale. It is hard enough to be worn safely in jewelry. But it is a difficult gem to facet.

Euclase was first found in the Ural Mountains in Russia. Today the most important source of gem-quality euclase is Brazil. Euclase can also be found in Australia, China, Zimbabwe, Austria, the United States, and other countries.

Evenkite has been found in France, Greenland, Hungary, Russia, and Slovakia.

EVENKITE

Evenkite is a very rare crystal. It belongs to a group of minerals called hydrocarbons. These minerals are made of only the elements carbon and hydrogen.

Evenkite is usually colorless or pale yellow. However, it will glow bright blue under UV light. Evenkite forms deep underground in hollow pockets inside rocks. It often forms as flat, plate-like crystals. These crystals may grow on top of other minerals.

VOLCANIC DISCOVERY

The name *evenkite* comes from the place where it was first found. It was discovered in the Evenkia district of Siberia in Russia in the early 1950s. It was found inside geodes within volcanic rock. Hot fluids in the rock left waxy material in the cavities. This slowly cooled and formed evenkite crystals.

Scientists have also found evenkite in other countries such as France and Slovakia. Evenkite has a rating of 1 on the Mohs scale. It is so soft that a person can easily scratch it with a fingernail.

FIRE AGATE

Fire agate is a gemstone made of two substances: iron oxide and a type of quartz called chalcedony agate. Fire agate formed millions of years ago because of volcanic activity. Hot water containing iron oxide seeped into cracks deep underground. As the water cooled, chalcedony was deposited in bubbly layers. Sometimes thin layers of iron oxide formed between them.

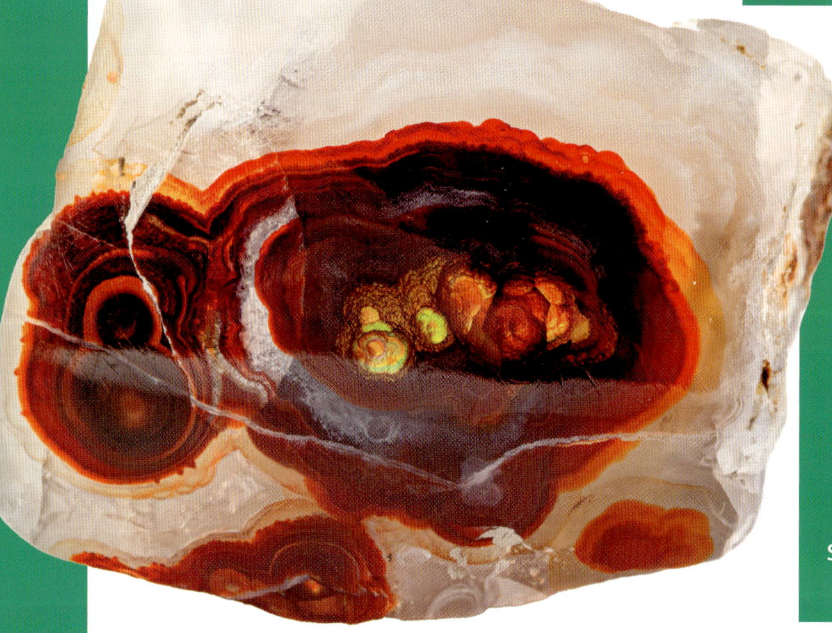

Fire agates may show flat layers similar to those of agates, but the layers may also appear to swirl or bubble. Their iridescent colors set fire agates apart from other stones.

These thin layers give fire agate its shimmering colors. When light hits the stone, it bounces between the layers. This creates flashes of red, orange, green, and even purple or blue. This effect is called iridescence. Fire agate is very rare.

HIDDEN FLAME

Fire agate was first discovered in 1939 in Arizona. In its natural condition, it looks like a plain brown rock. It took gem cutters a long time to learn how to shape and polish the stone so that the colors would shimmer. Today fire agate is found only in the desert regions of Arizona, Southern California, and central Mexico. It measures 6.5 to 7 on the Mohs scale.

Fluorite may show bands of color.

FLUORITE

Fluorite is a gemstone made from the compound calcium fluoride, which contains the element fluorine. Pure fluorite is clear. However, small amounts of other elements usually give fluorite some color. Violet is the most common color. But fluorite may also be yellow, green, blue, gray, or black. Fluorite will usually glow under UV light. The term *fluorescence* comes from this gemstone.

MORE THAN A GEM

The name *fluorite* comes from the Latin word *fluere*, which means "to flow." Fluorite melts easily. It is the main source of the element fluorine. Fluorine is part of fluoride, which is used in toothpaste to help protect teeth. Gem-quality fluorite can be found in many parts of the world, including Mexico, Canada, the United States, China, and many countries in Europe.

GARNET

Garnet refers to a group of gemstones made of many different minerals. All garnets have the same crystal structure and similar properties. However, each has a different combination of elements. There are more than 20 kinds of garnets. Each one is called a species. Only five species are commonly cut and used as gems.

Many people think of garnets as red. But garnets can be found in almost any color, including orange, yellow, purple, and green. Garnets are never found in a completely pure form. They are always mixed with other garnet species.

Spessartite garnet is an orange to reddish-brown species.

ANCIENT ADORNMENT

The name *garnet* comes from the Latin word for "pomegranate." These red stones resemble pomegranate seeds. Garnets have been used since ancient times. The Egyptians used garnets in their jewelry and carvings. Ancient Romans had special rings with garnets for stamping wax seals on documents. During the Middle Ages, both nobles and church leaders wore garnets. Today most of the world's garnets come from parts of Africa. This gem is the birthstone for January.

GRANDIDIERITE

Grandidierite is a very rare mineral that can be cut into beautiful gemstones. It is usually blue to green in color. Grandidierite has a trait called pleochroism. This means the brightness and shade of its color can change when viewed from different angles. Unlike some other gemstones, grandidierite is not heated to brighten or change its color. It is always shown in its natural state.

FROM ROCK TO GEM

Grandidierite is named after French explorer and naturalist Alfred Grandidier. The mineral was first discovered in 1902 off the southern coast of Madagascar. However, the deposit was small. In 2004, grandidierite crystals were discovered in Sri Lanka. In 2014, more crystals were discovered in Madagascar. Because of these finds, grandidierite can now be made into gemstones. Still, gem-quality grandidierite remains rare. Grandidierite has a hardness of 7.5 on the Mohs scale.

Many grandidierite specimens are too small to be cut into faceted gemstones.

Graphite may have a greasy feel due to how soft it is.

GRAPHITE

Graphite is a crystal made of pure carbon. It has the same chemical makeup as diamond, but its atoms do not form the same pattern. Unlike diamond, graphite is very soft. It is usually found as flakes or layers of crystals. Graphite is gray to black in

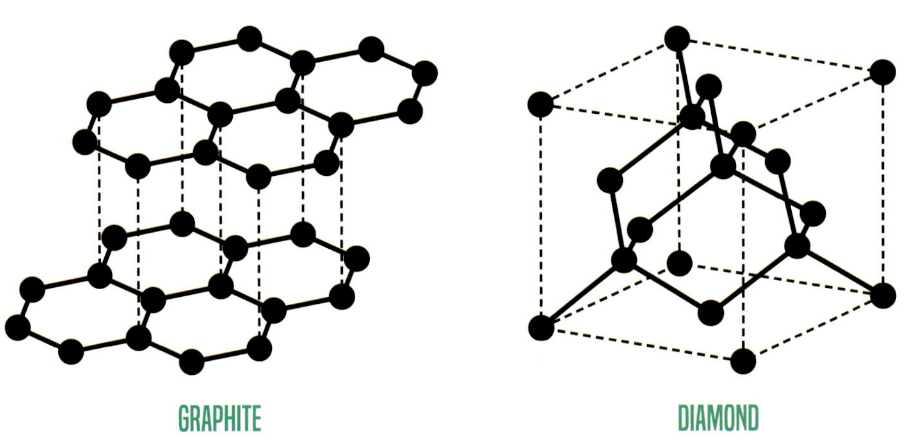

Carbon atoms in graphite form flat layers. The bonds between layers are weak, making graphite soft. In diamond, carbon atoms form a stronger three-dimensional shape.

color with a metallic shine. Because it looks like the metal lead, it is sometimes called black lead.

SOFT BUT USEFUL

Graphite was first discovered in northern England in the early 1500s. It was named in 1789 by German scientist Abraham Gottlob Werner. The name *graphite* comes from the Greek word *graphein*, which means "to write."

Even though it is soft, graphite is heat resistant. That makes it useful in rockets and airplanes. It also helps electricity flow, so it is used in batteries.

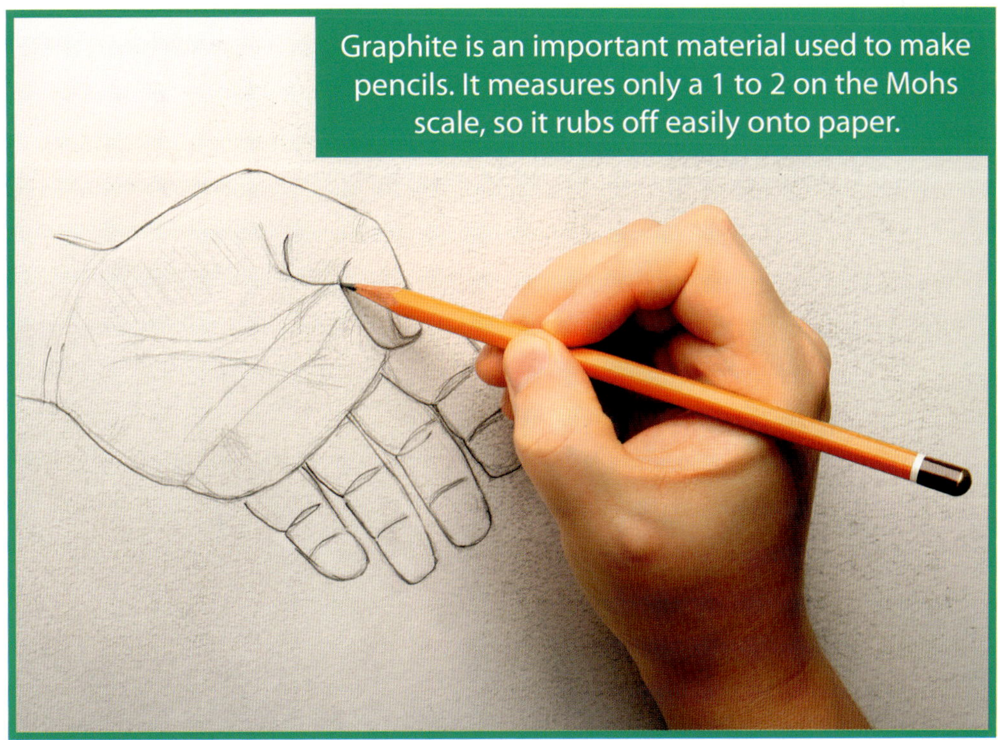

Graphite is an important material used to make pencils. It measures only a 1 to 2 on the Mohs scale, so it rubs off easily onto paper.

HELIODOR

Heliodor is a gemstone that comes from the same family as emerald and aquamarine. It is a type of beryl. It is known for being very clear and transparent. Its color can be yellow, orangish yellow, or greenish yellow. The yellow color comes from tiny amounts of iron inside the stone.

BRIGHT BEGINNINGS

Heliodor was discovered in 1910 in Namibia in the Rössing Mountains. The gem quickly gained attention for its bright, sunny color. The name *heliodor* comes from ancient Greek words that mean "gift from the Sun." Its name was inspired by old beliefs that golden gemstones held the power and warmth of the Sun.

The three major sources of heliodor are Brazil, Madagascar, and Namibia. Other countries that produce heliodor include Russia, Ukraine, and the United States. Heliodor has a hardness of 7.5 to 8 on the Mohs scale.

Heliodor crystals may show natural etching caused by high pressure during formation.

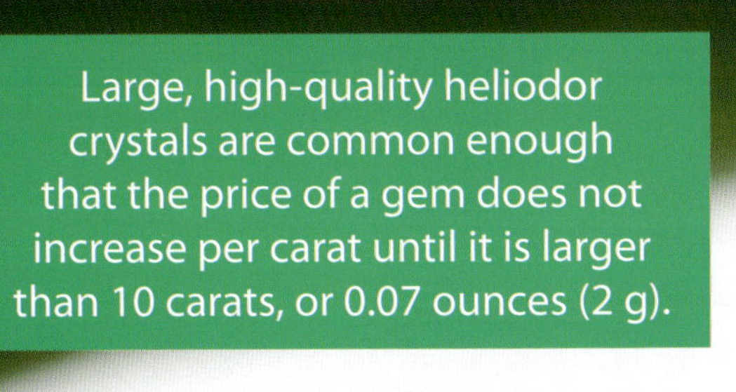
Large, high-quality heliodor crystals are common enough that the price of a gem does not increase per carat until it is larger than 10 carats, or 0.07 ounces (2 g).

Many idocrase gemstones show color zoning, with several colors or shades in a single crystal.

IDOCRASE

Idocrase comes in both gemstone and mineral forms. Most scientists use the name *idocrase* when talking about the gemstone. They use the name *vesuvianite* when talking about the mineral.

Idocrase usually forms in hot rock near magma. It forms clear, glass-like crystals with prism shapes. It can be green, yellowish green, bright yellow, or brownish green in color. Rare stones can be colorless, white, pink, blue, purple, red, or black.

FROM THE VOLCANO

In 1795, Abraham Gottlob Werner named the mineral vesuvianite. Crystals of the mineral were found near Mount Vesuvius, a volcano in Italy. The next year, in 1796, René-Just Haüy named it idocrase. This name comes from the Greek words *idos* and *krasis*, meaning "mixed appearance." This is because idocrase crystals can look different depending on how they form.

High-quality and brightly colored idocrase stones are popular with mineral collectors. Some stones are cut into gems or carved into small sculptures. Idocrase rates 6.5 on the Mohs scale.

Greenish-yellow idocrase gemstones are some of the most common and popular.

IOLITE

Iolite is made from the elements silicon, aluminum, iron, and magnesium. Iolite is a pleochroic gemstone. It displays three different colors when viewed from different angles. Violet iolites may display light violet, dark violet, and yellow-brown colors. Bluish iolites have a colorless, yellow, bluish-gray, and dark violet appearance.

Iolite is the gem-quality form of the mineral cordierite.

THE VIKINGS' STONE

In legends, iolite is called the Viking compass stone. Vikings are said to have used thin slices of iolite as a type of glare-reducing filter. They would hold up the iolite as they looked toward the sky. They could locate the position of the Sun, even on cloudy days. This would help them determine which direction to go.

Most iolite comes from India. However, other countries such as Tanzania, Brazil, and Sri Lanka also produce iolite. The gemstone has a hardness of 7 to 7.5 on the Mohs scale.

Jadeite is rarer and more expensive than nephrite.

JADEITE

Jadeite is one of two gemstones commonly referred to as jade. Nephrite also goes by the name *jade*. Jadeite is found in rocks that formed under high pressure. It comes in many colors, including green, yellow, pink, white, gray, black, brown, and light purple. The color in jadeite comes from trace elements in the stone, such as iron, chromium, and magnesium.

Jadeite gets its name from the Spanish phrase *piedra de ijada*. This means "stone of the side." Long ago, some people thought jadeite could help with kidney pain if it was rubbed on a person's side.

CULTURAL TREASURE

Jadeite is one of the world's oldest decorative stones. Artifacts made from jadeite have been found at ancient sites in Australia, Europe, Asia, and North and Central America. People have carved jadeite to make jewelry, vases, statues, tools, and weapons.

Jadeite can be found in many parts of the world. Countries where it is found include Myanmar, New Zealand, Canada, Taiwan, Russia, China, and many others. Jadeite ranges from 6.5 to 7 on the Mohs scale.

JASPER

Jasper is a type of quartz. It is made up of many microscopic quartz crystals mixed with other minerals. Because of these mixtures, jasper can come in almost any color. There are many kinds of jasper. Some names are based on how the stone looks. For example, leopard skin jasper has spots.

POWERS AND PROTECTION

The word *jasper* comes from the Latin word *iaspis*, meaning "spotted stone." People in ancient times used jasper in jewelry. Some people believed it had special powers. Some thought it

Jasper may be a solid color or have a pattern of spots, bands, swirls, or flower-like shapes.

could reveal lies. Others believed it had healing powers. Some even thought it could protect them against venomous animals.

Jasper remains popular in jewelry. It measures 7 on the Mohs scale. It is also used to make decorative objects. Jasper is found all over the world. However, certain colors and patterns can be found only in specific places.

SPIN AND SHINE

Rock tumbling is a way to smooth and polish rough stones. It uses water and abrasive grit. Grit might include tiny, rough grains of sand or other rocks to wear down the stones. The tumbler spins the rocks with the grit and water for several weeks. Together, they grind, smooth, and polish the stones. The process is similar to erosion, in which water and sand gradually wear down rocks. Jasper is one of the most popular stones used in rock tumbling.

Most jeremejevite
is pale in color.

JEREMEJEVITE

Jeremejevite is a rare crystal. It is made from the elements aluminum and boron. The crystals form deep underground. Jeremejevite is usually pale bluish green, blue, or yellowish brown. It can also be colorless.

BLUE TREASURE

Jeremejevite was discovered on Mount Soktui in Siberia, Russia, in 1883. It was called jeremejevite to honor a Russian scientist named Pavel Vladimirovich Eremeev. His last name was Jeremejev in German. At first, only microscopic grains of jeremejevite were found. These were too small to use as gemstones. Then, in 1973, large blue crystals were discovered in Namibia. These crystals were large enough to cut.

Today jeremejevite is rarely found in Russia. Namibia produces only small amounts. The stone is very rare. Jeremejevite has a hardness of 6.5 to 7.5 on the Mohs scale.

Collectors wanted large jeremejevite crystals for their mineral collections. Because of this, not many crystals were cut into gems.

LABRADORITE

Labradorite is a gemstone that forms from the mineral feldspar. It is best known for its colorful effect called labradorescence, a rainbow-like shimmer on the stone. Labradorescence is caused by light bending and bouncing through the different layers of the stone. This gives it a metallic shine.

Labradorite occurs in several varieties. These include transparent yellow, Oregon sunstone, and rainbow moonstone. Oregon sunstone may display a glittery effect caused by tiny minerals inside the stone.

AT HOME IN CANADA

Labradorite was named for Labrador, Canada, the place where it was discovered. Today it is found in many parts of the world. However, the most important sources are Labrador, Finland, and Madagascar. It has a hardness of 6 to 6.5 on the Mohs scale.

Labradorite shows flashes of blue, green, yellow, and red when viewed from different angles.

Rainbow moonstone
has a soft, colorful glow.

LAPIS LAZULI

Lapis lazuli is a blue gemstone. It is made up of several minerals, including lazurite, calcite, and pyrite. Its color ranges from deep violet blue to greenish blue. In the stone are tiny golden lines or flecks. These are made of pyrite, which is also known as fool's gold. Pyrite can make lapis lazuli more valuable. It gives the stone a unique sparkle that many people enjoy.

TREASURED FOR AGES

Lapis lazuli has been highly prized for thousands of years. People have found jewelry made from lapis lazuli in ancient tombs in Asia, Africa, and Europe. Beginning in the Middle Ages, it was ground into powder to make blue paint used by artists.

Lapis lazuli is still popular today. It has a hardness of 5 to 6 on the Mohs scale. It is mostly used in jewelry and carvings. For thousands of years, the finest lapis lazuli has come from the mountains of Afghanistan. Other major sources include Chile and Russia.

The blue color in lapis lazuli comes from lazurite.

Color variants and white streaks give each piece of larimar jewelry a unique look.

LARIMAR

Larimar is a blue gemstone that forms from the mineral pectolite. Its color ranges from sky blue to turquoise to greenish blue. The blue color comes from traces of copper in the stone. The finest stones are dark blue and slightly transparent. Larimar forms inside volcanic cavities when mineral-rich liquids mix under intense heat.

NAMED FOR THE SEA

Larimar is found only in the Dominican Republic. It was named by a man named Miguel Méndez. Méndez named the stone after his daughter. *Larimar* combines her name, Larissa, with *mar*, the Spanish word for "sea." Larimar ranks between 4.5 and 5 on the Mohs scale.

Larimar can have streaks of white that look like ripples in water. Because its colors look like the sea, it is sometimes called the dolphin stone.

LEGRANDITE

Legrandite is a rare, bright yellow gemstone. If it has clear crystals, they are usually small. As the crystals grow larger, they become more cloudy and less transparent. Legrandite contains the mineral arsenic. In its natural form, arsenic is toxic. This means it is not safe to eat or to breathe in. Experts suggest wearing gloves to touch the solid mineral.

Legrandite crystals are often found in sprays. These are arrangements of long, parallel crystals.

MINING LEGRANDITE

Legrandite was first discovered in the early 1930s. It was found in a mine in Nuevo León, Mexico. Legrandite was named after a mining engineer from Belgium with the last name Legrand. Other countries also produce legrandite. These include Namibia, Brazil, Japan, and the United States.

MALACHITE

Malachite is a gemstone made from copper. It can grow in several shapes. For example, it can form tiny needle-like crystals that are stuck together. It can also resemble round grape-like clusters. Malachite ranges in color from light green to almost black.

A TIMELESS GEM

People have used malachite for more than 3,000 years. In ancient Egypt, malachite was used to make jewelry, sculptures, and art. Malachite can also be easily ground to a powder. This made it a good coloring agent in ancient times.

Malachite is often found with light and dark bands.

Malachite can be found all over the world. In the 1800s, a copper mine near the Ural Mountains in Russia began producing large pieces of banded green malachite. Today most malachite comes from the Democratic Republic of the Congo in Africa. Smaller amounts are produced in Australia, France, and the United States.

Moldavite takes many different shapes, such as disks, spheres, and drops.

MOLDAVITE

Moldavite is a gemstone made of natural glass. It formed long ago when a meteorite crashed into Earth. The heat and force from the meteorite impact melted the nearby soil and rock into liquid glass. The glass was flung into the air. It cooled as it fell back to the ground. Moldavite ranges in color from brown to olive green to bright green.

SPACE STONE

Although many gemstones come from types of natural glass, moldavite comes from a specific event. Scientists believe it was created 14.7 million years ago when a giant meteorite struck southern Germany. This impact was so large that moldavite is found outside Germany as well. Today the main source of moldavite is the Czech Republic. In 1836, scientists named the gemstone after the Moldau River in the Czech Republic. The river is close to one of the major discovery sites. Moldavite has a hardness of 5 on the Mohs scale.

MOONSTONE

Moonstone is a gemstone made of two types of minerals: orthoclase and albite. These minerals mix together deep underground where it is very hot. As they cool, they separate into thin, flat layers. When light shines on the surface, it moves between the layers and spreads out in different directions. The light seems to roll across the stone and make it glow.

TOUCHED BY THE MOON

People have prized moonstones for thousands of years. The ancient Romans believed moonstones were formed from

The most valuable moonstones are clear with a glowing blue shine.

frozen moonlight. Others believed moonstones brought love and protection.

Moonstones are found in many places around the world. These include Sri Lanka, India, Australia, Mexico, Brazil, and the United States. Moonstones from India are known to be especially colorful.

Some musgravite stones can appear gray or colorless.

MUSGRAVITE

Musgravite is one of the rarest gemstones on Earth. It forms from the minerals magnesium and beryllium. Musgravite is closely related to another rare gemstone called taaffeite. Both have similar chemical structures. The only difference is how much magnesium they contain, with musgravite having a slightly lower amount of magnesium than taaffeite. Scientists must use high-powered instruments to tell them apart.

Musgravite's color can range from deep greenish blue to purple. Tiny amounts of other elements can affect the color. Musgravite bends and splits light in a way that makes it look very sparkly and colorful. This property is called dispersion.

A RARE GEMSTONE REVEALED

Musgravite gets its name from the Musgrave Ranges in Australia, where it was first discovered in 1967. At first it was mistaken for taaffeite. Finally, in 2005, studies confirmed that a new gemstone had been found. This made it even more valuable to collectors. Musgravite has also been found in Antarctica, Greenland, Tanzania, and Myanmar. Musgravite has a hardness of 8 to 8.5 on the Mohs scale.

The first musgravite crystal that was large enough to be cut and faceted was found in 1993.

OBSIDIAN

Obsidian is natural glass formed during volcanic eruptions. It is made of the same minerals as granite. However, it cools so quickly that crystals do not have time to form. Obsidian is usually black, dark green, or gray. But it can also appear yellow, red, greenish brown, or colorless. Sometimes two colors are swirled together in a single stone. The most common combination is black and brown.

Some obsidian forms at the surface as lava flows. However, the highest-quality obsidian forms underground. This obsidian is usually free of dirt or ash.

ANCIENT TOOL, MODERN TREASURE

Obsidian has been used for centuries to make tools, weapons, and decorative objects. Today it is used to make scalpel blades and other cutting tools as well as beautiful jewelry. It is found in locations worldwide where there has been recent volcanic activity. These include countries such as Argentina, Canada, Chile, Greece, Iceland, Japan, Kenya, Mexico, Russia, and the United States. Obsidian has a hardness of 5 to 5.5 on the Mohs scale.

ONYX

Onyx is a variety of chalcedony, a rock made of tiny quartz crystals. This gemstone is known for its parallel bands of color. While natural black onyx exists, it is rare. Most black onyx for sale has been dyed. Sometimes dye makes the bands of color stand out more. Other times, it makes the stone appear completely black. Onyx may also be dyed green, blue, pink, or white.

Onyx often shows bands in shades of black and white.

THROUGH THE AGES

Even in ancient times, people found a way to change the look of onyx. The ancient Romans darkened it using sugar water and acid. This method is still used today. Later, onyx became a popular gemstone for jewelry that people wore while mourning.

Over the centuries, people have shared some mysterious stories about these stones. Some people believed that onyx could help break up unhappy relationships. Others believed that black onyx helped release feelings of sorrow. Onyx is found all over the world. It rates 6.5 to 7 on the Mohs scale.

Common opals are usually solid colors such as gray, black, white, or brown.

OPAL

Opal is a gemstone that comes in two forms: precious opal and common opal. Precious opal can show any color of the rainbow. Common opal does not have this colorful display. This difference is because of how opals form. Instead of crystals, opal is made of microscopic spheres of a mineral called silicon dioxide. In precious opals, the spheres are the same size and stacked in a regular pattern. Light hits these spheres and bends, allowing people to see different colors in the gem. In common opals, the spheres are different sizes and do not have a uniform pattern.

A GEM OF LEGENDS

In ancient times, opal was a symbol of hope and purity. Later, people believed it had

Precious opals are often cut in cabochon shapes, which are smooth and domed instead of faceted.

special powers. Some people thought it could cure eye diseases or make someone invisible. Depending on the tradition, opals have been considered either lucky or unlucky.

Today opal comes mostly from Australia, Mexico, and the United States. Each location produces a specific type. Most of the world's precious opal comes from Australia. These opals are rarer than diamonds. The most valuable have a dark or black base. Opal has a hardness of 5 to 6.5 on the Mohs scale.

DID YOU KNOW?

Opalized wood has been petrified, or turned to stone over time. Most opalized wood is made of common opal. However, some pieces of petrified wood with precious opal have been found.

Opal can form a layer on top of petrified wood or replace the wood entirely during the process of petrification.

PAINITE

Painite is a gemstone formed from the mineral borate. It is red to brownish red in color. Painite resembles other gemstones such as almandines and rubies. For this reason, some cut painite has been mistaken for other gemstones in the past.

REDISCOVERED

Until recently, painite was considered to be the rarest gemstone in the world. The first painite was discovered in the early 1950s by a gemologist named Arthur Pain. He found it in Burma, which is now called Myanmar. For many years, only two crystals were known to exist. These were kept in the

The color of painite comes from small amounts of chromium and vanadium.

Natural History Museum in London. By 2001, only one more crystal had been found.

But in 2002, thousands of painite crystals were discovered in the Mogok region in Myanmar. Despite an increase in supply, most of these crystals are not suitable for cutting into gemstones. Even though there is now painite for sale, it is still a very rare gem. Painite measures 8 on the Mohs scale.

PARAÍBA TOURMALINE

Paraíba tourmaline is one of the most expensive gemstones in the world. It can be emerald green, turquoise, sky blue, bright blue, bluish violet, or purple. The mineral copper causes blue, turquoise, and green colors. Manganese causes violet and red tones.

A BRILLIANT BRAZILIAN DISCOVERY

Paraíba tourmalines are very rare. The stone was first discovered in the 1980s by Heitor Dimas Barbosa. He was looking for a new stone in the hills of Paraíba, Brazil. In 1989,

When cut into facets, Paraíba tourmalines appear to glow, even in very low light. Because of this, their color is often described as electric or neon.

the first handful of crystals was brought up out of the ground. For the next five years, people searched for more. But very little was found.

In 2000, similar tourmalines were discovered in Nigeria. A few years later, more were discovered in Mozambique. But most are not as bright or colorful as the stones in Brazil. Paraíba tourmalines from Brazil sell for much more than those from Nigeria or Mozambique. Paraíba tourmalines range from 7 to 7.5 on the Mohs scale.

Some animal rights activists question whether producing cultured pearls is ethical, since irritants may cause the mollusk pain.

PEARL

Pearls are made by mollusks such as clams and oysters. Sometimes a tiny irritant such as a grain of sand gets stuck in the shell. To protect itself, the mollusk coats the irritant in layers of hard, shiny material called nacre. Over time, this forms a pearl.

Pearl is the only gemstone made by animals. But not all pearls form naturally. Cultured pearls start when a person puts a tiny bead or piece of shell inside a mollusk to start the pearl formation process. Cultured pearls are most common today.

Pearls come in many colors. The most common are white and cream. Other colors of pearls include black, gray, silver, pink, green, purple, and blue.

DID YOU KNOW?

Mother-of-pearl is made of the same substance as pearls. It forms an inner layer on mollusk shells. Mother-of-pearl is widely used in jewelry. However, it is not considered a gemstone.

TREASURE OF THE SEA

People have valued pearls for thousands of years. A Chinese historian wrote about them in about 2200 BCE. Natural pearls are found in ponds, lakes, and oceans. Cultured pearls can also come from freshwater or saltwater mollusks. Most cultured freshwater pearls come from China. Today natural saltwater pearls come mostly from the coasts of Australia, the Philippines, Indonesia, and Bahrain.

Pearls are soft compared with other gemstones. They range between 2.5 and 4.5 on the Mohs scale. Still, they are popular in necklaces, bracelets, rings, and earrings. Pearl is a birthstone for June.

Pearl necklaces often feature these gems strung together as beads.

PERIDOT

Peridot comes from the mineral olivine. It can be yellowish green, olive, or brownish green. The green color comes from iron in the mineral itself. For this reason, peridot is never found in other colors.

Most peridot forms deep inside Earth's mantle. It is brought to the surface by volcanoes. It appears as round rocks with crystals inside. Sometimes peridot is found in meteorites that have fallen to Earth.

Gem miners find peridot in lava flows.

A LONG HISTORY

The use of peridot in jewelry dates back to 2000 BCE. The ancient Egyptians found peridot on a small volcanic island in the Red Sea. They called it the gem of the Sun. In Hawaii, peridot was believed to be the tears of the volcano goddess. In the Middle Ages, Europeans decorated cathedrals with peridot.

Most of the world's peridot comes from the San Carlos Apache Reservation in Arizona. In the 1990s, new deposits were discovered in Pakistan. Other sources include China and Africa.

Phenakite is prized for its clarity. Gems with inclusions are usually worth less than those that appear clear.

PHENAKITE

Phenakite is a type of mineral. When cut and polished into a gemstone, it resembles quartz. Some phenakite is colorless. It can also be pale yellow, pink, or brown. Polished phenakite appears bright. However, cut stones are rare and are usually kept in special gem collections.

Phenakite comes from the Ural Mountains of Russia and the Northern Cape province of South Africa. In the United States, there are deposits of phenakite in Maine and Colorado. It is also found in Tanzania, Sri Lanka, Zambia, Madagascar, and many countries in Europe.

MISTAKEN IDENTITY

Phenakite's name comes from the ancient Greek word *phenakos*, which means "deceiver." This is because it was often mistaken for quartz or diamonds. Phenakite was first named in 1833.

Geologists can easily tell the difference between phenakite and diamond. But when phenakite is set in jewelry, it is harder to tell the difference. Phenakites can look like low-quality diamonds. Phenakite ranks 7.5 to 8 on the Mohs scale.

Large phenakite crystals are rare. The price per carat rises for larger gems.

POUDRETTEITE

Poudretteite is one of the rarest gemstones in the world. It contains the elements potassium, sodium, boron, silicon, and oxygen. Poudretteite forms clear crystals. Its colors range from pink to violet. Some stones appear almost colorless. Others have strong, bright colors that make them very valuable to collectors.

One of the largest faceted poudretteite gemstones is slightly more than 9 carats, or 0.06 ounces (1.7 g).

TINY CRYSTALS, BIG DISCOVERY

Poudretteite was named after the Poudrette family. The Poudrettes own and operate a quarry near Mont Saint-Hilaire in Canada, where the mineral was first found. A few tiny crystals were discovered in the 1960s. These were not large enough to be cut into gemstones. Poudretteite was not officially recognized as a new mineral until 1986.

In 2000, the first gem-quality poudretteite was found in Myanmar. This discovery greatly increased interest in the gem. Poudretteite ranges from 5 to 6 on the Mohs scale.

PREHNITE

Prehnite is a mineral that can be used as a gemstone. Prehnite mostly forms in volcanic rock. The rock changes over time because of heat and pressure or from hot water moving deep underground.

Prehnite's colors can include pale green, green, bluish green, yellowish green, and yellow. Completely transparent prehnite is rare. But it sometimes is found in crystals from Quebec, Canada.

Prehnite forms as masses or globs more often than as crystals.

Most prehnite that is cut into gemstones comes from Australia. These are usually yellow to green in color.

THE FIRST NAMESAKE GEM

Prehnite was the first gemstone named for a person. It was named after Colonel Hendrik Von Prehn. He discovered the mineral in 1774 in South Africa. Today prehnite is found in other countries around the world. These include France, Italy, Germany, Russia, the Czech Republic, New Zealand, and the United States. Prehnite has a hardness of 6 to 6.5 on the Mohs scale.

Rose quartz is a popular variety of quartz. Darker, more intensely pink stones are more valuable than lighter ones.

QUARTZ

Quartz is a gemstone made of the elements silicon and oxygen. About 20 percent of Earth's crust is quartz. Quartz can form in all kinds of rocks at any temperature. It does not break down easily. When rocks wear away, quartz is left behind. This is why quartz often forms sand. Most of the sand on beaches, in rivers, and in deserts is made of quartz.

The crystals in quartz are usually clear or white. But trace elements can create a variety of colors. These include gray, purple, yellow, green, pink, red, brown, and black. Quartz comes in many varieties. Some of these include amethyst, jasper, citrine, and agate.

SO MANY USES

People have used quartz for thousands of years. Its wide range of patterns and colors makes it one of the most popular gemstones. Even today, quartz is one of the most widely used minerals. One of its most common uses is in glass. Windows, drinking glasses, and eyeglasses can all be made of quartz. Quartz can be found in all parts of the world. It has a hardness of 7 on the Mohs scale.

One rare type of quartz shows inclusions of dumortierite, a blue mineral.

REALGAR

Realgar is a mineral that forms bright orangish-red crystals. It is very soft, measuring only 1.5 to 2 on the Mohs scale. Realgar is also unstable. When it is exposed to light, it starts to change into a different mineral called pararealgar. Over time, it can break down into a powder. It should be stored in a dark, closed container. Another reason to be careful with realgar is that it contains arsenic, which is poisonous.

DID YOU KNOW?

During the Middle Ages, people realized realgar was poisonous. They began using it to kill rodents, insects, and weeds.

Realgar is too soft to be cut into gemstones.

Realgar is often found near orpiment, a yellow mineral that forms as realgar decays.

COLORFUL BUT TOXIC

The name *realgar* comes from an Arabic word meaning "powder of the mine." People have used realgar for thousands of years. People in ancient China used it to make decorations. But over time, the mineral fell apart. Many of these carvings are damaged.

Because it is so soft, realgar can be ground into powder. It was used to color paints, inks, and dyes. Today realgar is found around the world.

RED BERYL

Red beryl is one of the rarest and most expensive gemstones. For red beryl to form, conditions must be just right. First, enough of the element beryllium must be present. The mineral manganese must be available at the same time and location. This mineral gives the gemstone its red color. Third, the right mix of other elements, including aluminum, silicon, and oxygen, must be present. As these are heated by lava, they move into cracks in rock where they mix with water.

For gem-quality red beryl to form, these cracks must have enough space for crystals to grow.

UTAH'S FIERY GEM

Another name for red beryl is bixbite. In 1904, Maynard Bixby discovered red beryl in the Thomas Range in Utah. In 1912, the stone was named bixbite in Bixby's honor. Today red beryl is found in only three places in the world. These are the Wah Wah Mountains and the Thomas Range in Utah and the Black Range in New Mexico. Only the red beryl in the Wah Wah Mountains is high quality enough to facet into gems.

Red beryl has a hardness of 7.5 to 8 on the Mohs scale. It would make a strong stone for jewelry. However, most red beryl is bought by mineral collectors and never cut.

RHODOCHROSITE

Rhodochrosite is a gemstone formed from the element manganese. It is created when hot water underground dissolves manganese and carries it through the earth. The manganese combines with a material called carbonate, creating a new mineral. The water flows through cracks. It drips from the ceilings of caves deep underground. Over time, these drips harden into stalactites made of rhodochrosite crystals. Inside are beautiful layers of reds and pinks. They may also have yellows and browns.

Rhodochrosite often reveals ring-like layers when cut open due to how it forms.

The most famous of all rhodochrosite crystals is orangish red. This gemstone is called the Alma King. It is 5.5 by 6.5 inches (14 by 16.5 cm) in size.

FROM ROMANIA TO THE ROCKIES

Rhodochrosite was first discovered in 1813 in silver mines in present-day Romania. Today it is also found in Argentina, South Africa, and Peru. The biggest and most famous rhodochrosite crystals have been found near Alma, Colorado.

Rhodochrosite is often used as a stone for carvings. It is a soft stone with a hardness of 3.5 to 4 on the Mohs scale. Some legends say that wearing rhodochrosite brings compassion, joy, and creativity.

Rhodonite is often found in massive forms. These appear as large, solid chunks rather than crystals.

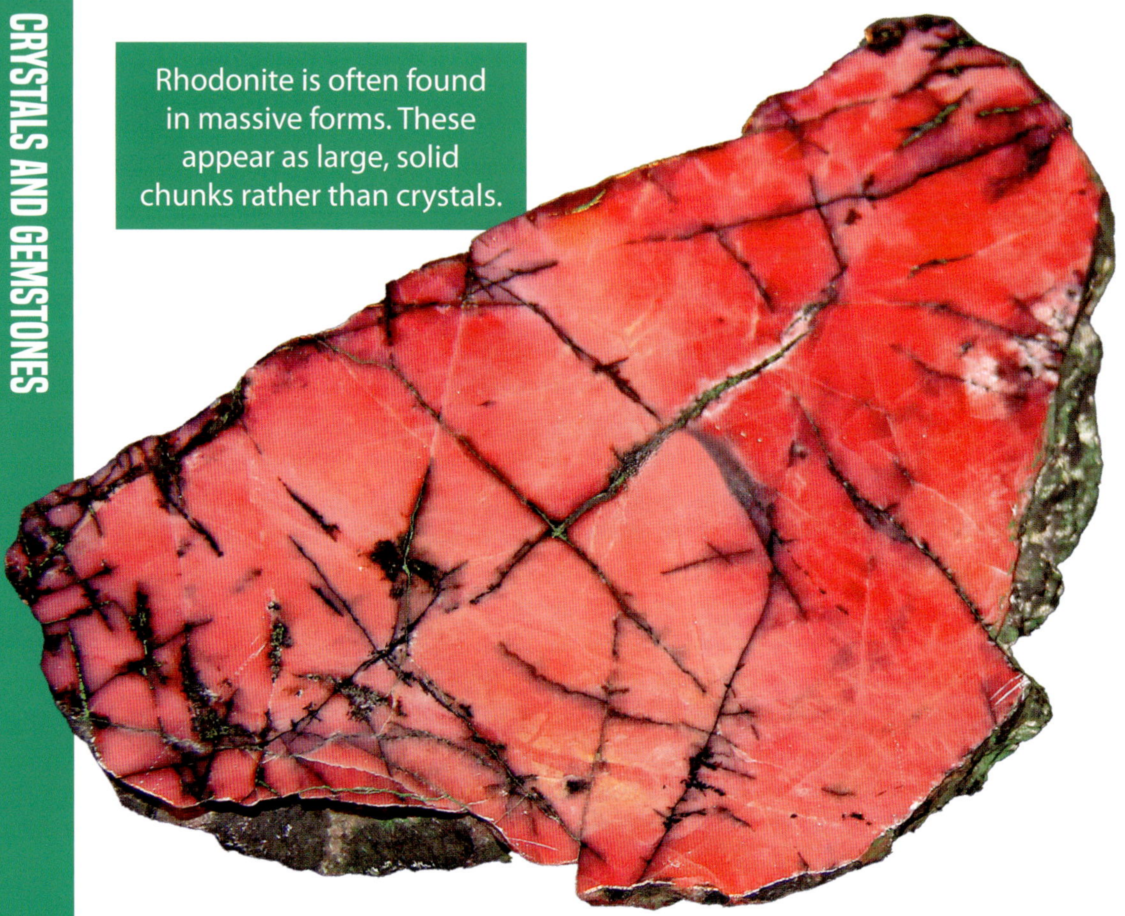

RHODONITE

Rhodonite is a gemstone formed from the mineral manganese. It ranges in color from pink to rosy red. It may also include shades of brownish red. Many pieces display black veins caused by manganese oxide.

THE ROSE-COLORED STONE

Rhodonite is a popular material for jewelry and decorative objects. However, it is one of the most difficult gemstones to cut because of its structure. It has a hardness of 6 on the Mohs scale.

Rhodonite is found in Russia, Canada, Australia, Japan, the United States, and other countries. It was named in 1819 by Christoph Friedrich Jasche. The name comes from the Greek word for "rose" because of the gem's color.

Gem carvers commonly make beads, figurines, and other objects from rhodonite instead of cut gemstones.

RUBY

Ruby is one of the most valuable gemstones in the world. It is the red variety of corundum. All rubies are medium to dark red in color. The color comes from traces of the mineral chromium. Chromium also causes fluorescence. Some rubies glow so brightly that the fluorescence can be seen in natural sunlight, not just in UV light.

PRIZED FOR MILLENNIA

Rubies have been prized for thousands of years. Myanmar has been an important source of rubies since 600 CE. Rubies from Myanmar usually bring the highest prices. They are famous for their deep bloodred color with purplish hues. These rubies are known as pigeon's blood rubies.

Today rubies are mined all around the world. Besides Myanmar, rubies are found in Vietnam, Thailand, India, parts of the Middle East, eastern Africa, and the United States. Ruby is the birthstone for July. Besides being used for jewelry, rubies are used to make lasers, watches, and medical instruments.

The name *ruby* is derived from the Latin word *ruber*, which means "red."

Ruby rates 9 on the Mohs scale. It is hard enough for daily wear in jewelry. Diamond is the only harder natural gemstone.

SAPPHIRE

Sapphire is a variety of the gemstone corundum. Sapphire's best-known color is blue. But sapphires are not only blue. They come in every color except red. Red corundum is known as ruby. Sapphires can be violet, green, yellow, orange, pink, or purple. These other colors of sapphire are often called fancy sapphires. Trace elements such as iron, copper, and magnesium give these sapphires their color. There is also a sapphire that looks blue in daylight but purple under artificial lights.

BEAUTIFUL AND STRONG

In ancient Greece and Rome, people believed that blue sapphires protected them from envy and harm. During the Middle Ages, blue sapphires symbolized Christianity's heaven.

Sapphire is the birthstone for September.

Sapphires today are used in scientific instruments, electronics, and watches. They can be found in countries throughout the world. These include Tanzania, Myanmar, Russia, the United States, China, Brazil, and Australia.

STAR STONE

A star sapphire is a type of sapphire. It shows a special reflection. Light forms a star shape that seems to be trapped inside the stone. This gemstone trait is known as asterism. Rubies, spinel, and garnets can display the star pattern too.

Most star sapphires have six rays. Very rare stones have 12.

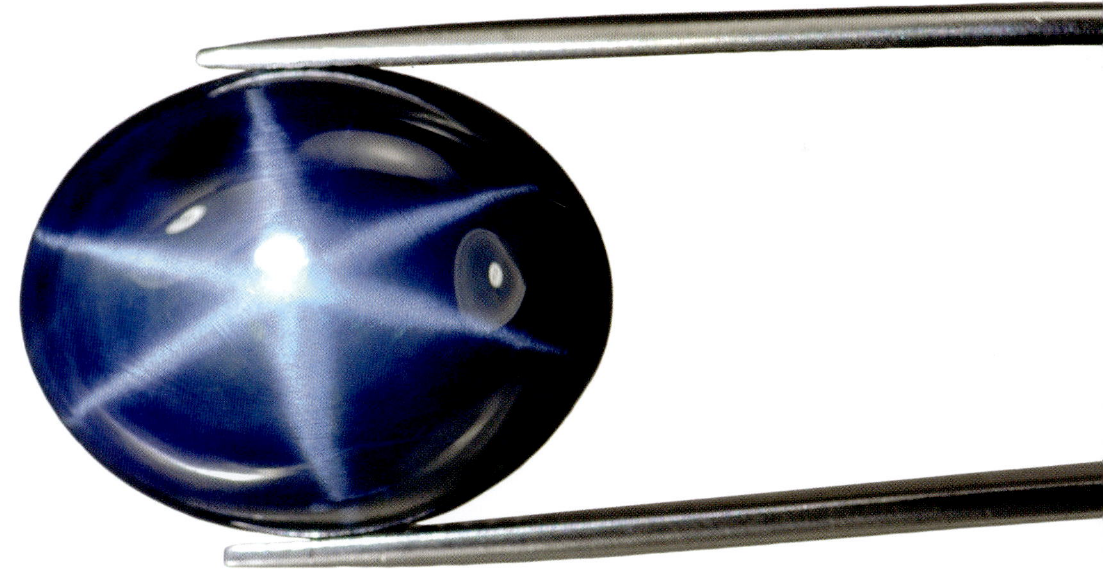

The name *scapolite* comes from the Greek word *skapos*, meaning "rod." This is because it often forms long, rod-shaped crystals.

SCAPOLITE

Scapolite is a gemstone that forms from aluminum, sodium, and calcium. It can grow in different types of rocks, including volcanic rocks. Scapolite is usually yellow, orange, pink, or violet. When cut a certain way, it can show a trait called chatoyancy. This is when light reflects off the surface to form a line that moves across the stone. This is also called the cat's-eye effect.

Some scapolite can glow under UV light. A type called rainbow scapolite can also show iridescence. This means it shines with colors that change in the light.

FROM MINERAL TO GEMSTONE

In 1913, the first gem-quality crystals were discovered in Myanmar. These crystals were white, pink, and violet. In 1920, yellow scapolite was found in Madagascar. Later, people uncovered more crystals in Brazil and Mozambique. Other sources include Kenya, Tanzania, Canada, China, India, and Pakistan. Scapolite has a hardness of 5.5 to 6 on the Mohs scale.

SCHEELITE

Scheelite is a mineral that is a major source of the element tungsten. Some scheelite crystals can be cut into gemstones. Scheelite comes in many colors. These include yellow, orange, brown, green, violet, red, white, and gray. Some scheelite crystals are colorless. If scheelite is cut just right, it can shine brightly and sparkle with flashes of rainbow colors. This sparkling effect is called fire.

Scheelite is a fairly common mineral, although it is rarely gem quality.

Scheelite is fluorescent. It usually glows sky blue to bluish white under UV light. Some people use UV lamps at night to search for it. They can see its bright blue glow.

HANDLE WITH CARE

Scheelite was named after the Swedish chemist C. W. Scheele. It can be found in Austria, Italy, Brazil, Rwanda, and the United States. Scheelite rates 4.5 to 5 on the Mohs scale. Because these gemstones are not very hard, they should be handled carefully if used in jewelry.

SCORODITE

Scorodite is a colorful mineral that forms in crystals. It comes in many colors, including green, blue, bluish green, gray, grayish green, yellowish brown, and violet. Some pieces are nearly colorless. Scorodite may look bluish green in daylight but change to bluish purple or grayish blue under lamplight.

SCENTED SCORODITE

Scorodite was named in 1818 by Johann Friedrich August Breithaupt. The name comes from the Greek word for garlic. Scorodite gives off a garlic-like smell when heated. The smell comes from the arsenic it contains.

Small amounts of scorodite can be found all over the world. Some of the best-known sources are Germany, the Czech Republic, Austria, England, and Algeria. Very large crystals have been discovered in Namibia, Mexico, Brazil, and Japan.

Scorodite measures 3.5 to 4 on the Mohs scale. Because of this, it is rarely cut into gemstones.

SERANDITE

Serandite is a very rare gemstone. It contains the mineral manganese. This gives it a salmon pink color. It can also appear in shades of red, orange, dark orange, or brown. Some crystals are colorless.

Its unique range of colors makes serandite a favorite among collectors.

QUEBEC'S CLAIM

The main source of serandite is Mont Saint-Hilaire in Quebec, Canada. So far, this is the only location that has produced crystals suitable for cutting into gemstones. Even so, it is not easy to find crystals that can be used in jewelry.

Serandite has a hardness of 4.5 to 5.5 on the Mohs scale. Because it is so soft, it needs a protective setting to reduce scratches if used in jewelry. However, serandite is still popular among mineral collectors. Serandite is found in a few other locations across the globe. These include the United States, Russia, Japan, and South Africa. Even in these places, serandite is still considered a rare and prized mineral.

Lizardite is the most common serpentine.

SERPENTINE

Serpentine is the name for a group of gemstones. This group includes antigorite, chrysotile, and lizardite. They range in color from pale green to dark green, yellow, and even black. Some stones are colorless. They are all made of the same elements but have different properties. Since the members of this group are not always easy to tell apart, they may just be referred to as serpentine. Serpentine always occurs in huge formations.

SNAKE-LIKE STONE

The name *serpentine* comes from the Latin word *serpens*, meaning "snake." These gemstones' splotchy green appearances resemble some snakes. The gem rates between 3 and 6 on the Mohs scale. Serpentine can be found in England, Scotland, Italy, Japan, Canada, and the United States. In 1965, it was named the state rock of California.

SPHALERITE

Sphalerite is a colorful crystal that is sometimes used as a gemstone. It is also the main source of the metal zinc. Sphalerite forms deep underground in cracks and cavities. It comes in a wide variety of colors, including black, brown, yellow, red, green, and light blue. Some sphalerites are clear and have no color at all. These can sparkle with rainbow flashes of color, called fire.

Sphalerite is also called blackjack or zinc blende.

LEAD IMPOSTER

The name *sphalerite* comes from a Greek word that means "treacherous" or "deceiving." This is because darker types of sphalerite can look like galena. Galena is a kind of lead.

Sphalerite is mined in many places. The top producers include Australia, Bolivia, Canada, China, Mexico, Peru, and the United States. Sphalerite has a hardness of 3.5 to 4 on the Mohs scale. This means it is too fragile for most jewelry. It can chip or break easily. However, it is a popular gem among collectors. Sphalerite is also mined for its zinc.

Sphene grows in wedge-shaped crystals.

SPHENE

Sphene is a gemstone also known as titanite. Sphene comes in many different colors. These include yellow, orange, red, brown, green, gray, and black. The amount of iron in the gem affects its color. Yellow and green gemstones have a small amount of iron. Brown and black stones have more iron. Sphene is pleochroic. This means that some sphene shows different colors depending on how it is viewed.

NAME SWAP

The name *sphene* comes from the Greek word *sphenos*, meaning "wedge." This is because of the shape of its crystals. In 1982, the International Mineralogical Association changed this mineral's name to *titanite*. However, *sphene* is still the name used in the gem and jewelry industries. Countries where it can be found include the United States, Ukraine, Zimbabwe, Madagascar, the United Kingdom, and Ireland. Sphene has a hardness of 5 to 5.5 on the Mohs scale.

Similarly to diamonds, sphene can split white light to show different colors. This is called dispersion. Dispersion makes the gemstone sparkle.

SPINEL

Spinel is a gemstone that comes in a wide range of colors. These include red, pink, yellow, purple, blue, and bluish green. Reds and pinks are caused by traces of chromium. Orange and purple stones get their color from a combination of iron and chromium. Bright blues are colored by traces of cobalt.

SPINEL'S ROYAL SECRET

Spinel is sometimes called the great imposter. In ancient times, mines in central and Southeast Asia produced very large spinel crystals. These were called Balas rubies. Some of these stones

Spinel is often mistaken for other colorful gemstones, especially ruby.

were treasured by royalty. Some of the world's most famous rubies in crowns and religious jewelry were actually spinel. The gemstone was not correctly identified until the late 1700s.

The two best-known sources for spinel are Myanmar and Sri Lanka. Spinel is also found in other countries. These include Vietnam, Madagascar, Tanzania, Tajikistan, and Mozambique.

THE BLACK PRINCE'S RUBY

The Black Prince's Ruby is a gemstone named after Edward of Woodstock, known as the Black Prince. It is one of the most famous gems in the world. It weighs about 170 carats, or 1.2 ounces (34 g). It is set in the Imperial State Crown, the royal crown worn by English monarchs. However, the stone is not a ruby. It is a red spinel.

The name *spodumene* is from the Greek word *spodumenos*, which means "ash colored." This references the crystal's usual shade of gray.

SPODUMENE

Spodumene is a type of crystal. It is usually a dull, gray color. Gray spodumene is rarely used for gemstones. However, there are colorful types of spodumene that can be cut into beautiful gems. The colors can range from transparent white to yellow, green, pink, and purple. Pink spodumene is known as kunzite.

The green gemstones are called hiddenite. Hiddenite is the rarest kind of spodumene gemstone. There are also blue spodumene crystals. But these fade when exposed to light. For this reason, they are mostly kept by collectors.

FINDING SPODUMENE

Spodumene crystals are found throughout the world. Yellow spodumene is found in Brazil and Afghanistan. Hiddenite was first found in North Carolina. Spodumene is also found in Madagascar and Myanmar.

Kunzite comes mainly from Afghanistan.

SUGILITE

Sugilite is a mineral that can be cut and polished into a gemstone. Its purple color comes from an element called manganese. Sugilite is often found in massive forms instead of crystals. The most important factor in deciding the value of this stone is its color. The deepest color receives the highest value.

NEW VALUE

Sugilite was discovered in 1944 by a Japanese geologist named Ken-ichi Sugi. Sugilite is named in his honor. Sugi discovered the mineral in southwestern Japan. It was made up of tiny yellow crystals. It had no value as a gemstone. Then, in 1955, dark pink crystals were found in central India. However, this

Sugilite stones having light areas mixed with dark purple are lower in value than those of uniform color.

material also wasn't able to be cut. In 1975, sugilite was discovered in South Africa. It had enough manganese to give it a deep purple color. This became the first source of gem-quality sugilite.

Sugilite has a hardness of 6 to 6.5 on the Mohs scale. It can be made into jewelry. Sugilite may also be carved into decorative objects.

Sugilite is sometimes carved into beads for jewelry.

Inclusions reflect light and make sunstone sparkle. Very small pieces of minerals create a reddish or golden glow on the surface.

SUNSTONE

Sunstone is a gemstone that comes from the mineral feldspar. Its name comes from its sunny appearance. It can range in color from pale yellow to reddish orange or brown. Some sunstones have shiny pieces of other minerals inside, such as hematite or copper.

SACRED AND SHINY

People have used sunstone for hundreds of years. Sunstone was once rare and expensive. Eventually larger amounts of the gemstone were found in Norway, Siberia, and other places, making it less costly. In the early 1900s, Americans discovered sunstone in Oregon.

American Indian artifacts featuring sunstone show this gem had been in use long before it was mined to be sold. One legend tells of a warrior whose blood fell on pieces of Oregon sunstone. This gave the stone a sacred power.

Today Oregon produces several kinds of sunstone, including some unique to the state. Sunstone is also mined in India, Mexico, China, Namibia, and Madagascar. Sunstone measures 6 to 7 on the Mohs scale.

Sunstone is from the same family of feldspar minerals as moonstone. Sunstone is warmer in color and has a different type of sparkle.

TAAFFEITE

Taaffeite is a very rare gemstone. It can appear lilac, mauve, brown, red, or bluish green. It is found in rocks that have changed over time because of heat and pressure. It has also been found as smooth pebbles in riverbeds or as microscopic crystals. Taaffeite is formed from the same minerals as musgravite. The main difference between the two gemstones is the amount of magnesium each one contains.

Taaffeite, *bottom left*, is one of several rare gemstones.

A CHANCE DISCOVERY

Taaffeite was first discovered in 1945 by gemologist Richard Taaffe. He found it in a jeweler's collection of spinel gemstones. Today taaffeite is found in Sri Lanka, Myanmar, Tanzania, Sweden, and China. It has a hardness of 8 to 8.5 on the Mohs scale.

TANZANITE

Tanzanite is a gemstone that forms from the mineral zoisite. It displays pleochroism, showing different colors from different angles. These colors are blue, violet, and yellowish green or brown. Heat removes or reduces the yellowish-green and brown colors, bringing out the blue to violet colors. In nature, this can happen slowly from the Sun's heat, but it is rare. Today almost all tanzanite for sale is heat treated.

JUST ONE PLACE ON EARTH

Tanzanite gets its name from Tanzania, where it was first unearthed. It was discovered in 1967 in the Merelani hills near Mount Kilimanjaro. This remains the only place in the world where tanzanite is found. Some reports say it was discovered by a Maasai person, a member of an Indigenous group in Tanzania. Others say it was discovered by a miner. Tanzanite has a hardness of 6 to 7 on the Mohs scale.

Tanzanite is one of the birthstones for December.

The element vanadium causes the violet-blue color of tanzanite.

Most tektite is glossy black. It may also be green or yellow.

TEKTITE

Tektite is a natural glass formed when a meteorite struck Earth long ago. The impact was so strong that some parts of Earth's surface were heated into molten rock. Droplets of this molten material flew through the atmosphere. They quickly cooled in the air and became solid shapes. These include spheres, teardrops, disks, and rods.

ANCIENT GLASS

The name *tektite* comes from the Greek word *tektos*, which means "melted." People in ancient China wrote about tektite in about 900 BCE. It was first described in scientific literature in

1788. Later, tektite was discovered in Texas. These stones were called bediasites after the Bedias people, American Indians who once lived in the area.

For hundreds of years, people did not know much about tektite. But during the 1900s, more tektite sources were found. Scientists around the world began researching this gemstone. Tektite has a hardness of 5 to 6.5 on the Mohs scale.

Yellow tektite comes from the deserts of Libya.

TIGEREYE

Tigereye is a gemstone formed from the minerals quartz and crocidolite. It is created through a process called the crack-seal mechanism. This cycle starts when a quartz rock cracks. Mineral-rich water flows into the crack. Quartz forms along the surface of the crack. If the rock contains crocidolite, crocidolite crystals form along these pieces. This process repeats, with more cracks forming and being filled. Iron from the crocidolite creates the well-known shades of brown and gold that turn the material into tigereye.

DID YOU KNOW?

Sometimes crocidolite is not stained by iron. It keeps its original blue color. These stones are called hawk's-eye.

The parallel bands that result from tigereye's formation are visible in unpolished stones.

Tigereye is often polished to make beads, jewelry, and decorative items.

A GOLDEN GLOW

Quartz and crocidolite crystals have different structures. The way they form next to one another creates a feature called chatoyancy. A band of light seems to move through the stone. This effect is what gives tigereye its name.

Tigereye can be found in countries around the world. These include Australia, Tanzania, Ukraine, Madagascar, China, South Africa, the United Kingdom, and the United States. It has a hardness of 7 on the Mohs scale.

Natural blue topaz is rare. Today colorless topaz can be turned sky blue with heat and radiation. This also causes darker colors.

TOPAZ

Topaz is a gemstone made of the elements aluminum and fluorine. Topaz forms in a type of rock called pegmatite. This rock forms where magma reaches Earth's surface. Some stones are clear. Topaz also comes in a variety of colors. The different colors are caused by different elements. Golden yellow and blue are common. Rare colors include pink, red, and reddish orange.

FROM MAGIC MYTHS TO ROYAL RINGS

Ancient Egyptians believed topaz was colored by the glow of the Sun god, Ra. Ancient Greeks believed topaz could increase strength or make someone invisible. Russian royalty wore topaz in jewelry, leading to the name imperial topaz.

Brazil is the main source of gem-quality topaz. But it can also be found in other countries, including Russia, Pakistan, the United States, Mexico, and Australia. Topaz has a hardness of 8 on the Mohs scale.

DID YOU KNOW?

The heaviest faceted gemstone is a topaz. This stone is called the El Dorado Topaz. It weighs 31,000 carats, which is about 13.7 pounds (6.2 kg).

Imperial topaz is usually orangish pink to pinkish red.

TOURMALINE

Tourmaline comes in almost every color of the rainbow. It has one of the widest color ranges of any gem. Tourmalines can be rich red, pink, green, yellow, blue, or violet. The colors are caused by different minerals in the stone. Iron produces greens and blues. Manganese causes reds and pinks. Some tourmalines show two or more colors in one stone. Black tourmaline is deep brown to bluish black.

Some tourmaline crystals show multiple colors. The name *tourmaline* comes from the Sri Lankan words *tura mali*, meaning "stone of mixed colors."

Black tourmaline makes up about 95 percent of all tourmaline. However, most of it isn't gemstone quality.

MISTAKEN BUT MAGNIFICENT

People have likely used tourmaline as a gem for centuries. However, it was probably mistaken for stones such as ruby or emerald at times. Brazil is one of the world's main sources of tourmaline. Other producing countries include Afghanistan, the United States, Mozambique, Nigeria, and Pakistan.

Turquoise often includes dark veins. These are made of the surrounding rock from its formation.

TURQUOISE

Turquoise is a gemstone found in dry areas. It forms when water rich in copper seeps into the ground. The water reacts with minerals that contain the elements phosphorus and aluminum. Turquoise ranges from shades of blue to bluish green to yellowish green. The color depends on the minerals in the stone. Copper gives turquoise its deep blue color. Gemstones with darker shades of blue and less green are usually more valuable.

ANCIENT BEAUTY, MODERN MEANING

The name *turquoise* comes from French words meaning "Turkish stone." Turquoise probably first arrived in France from Turkey. People in different cultures have prized this stone for more than 5,000 years. Rulers in ancient Egypt wore turquoise jewelry. Later, people in ancient Chinese and American Indian cultures did the same. Indigenous peoples in Mexico have too.

Turquoise is also the national gem of Tibet. Some people there believe turquoise helps bring health, good luck, and protection.

A SMOOTH FINISH

Turquoise is often formed into cabochons. A cabochon is a gemstone that has been shaped and polished instead of cut into facets. A cabochon usually has a smooth, rounded surface and a flat base. Cabochons may be any shape, but oval is the most common.

Since about 200 BCE, American Indian peoples in the southwestern United States have used turquoise.

WILLEMITE

Willemite is a gemstone that forms from the mineral zinc. It grows as small crystals that are pale green, yellow, or colorless. Larger crystals may be pale green, dark green, reddish brown, or even black. Some willemite is fluorescent. Some stones continue to glow after the light has been removed. This is known as phosphorescence.

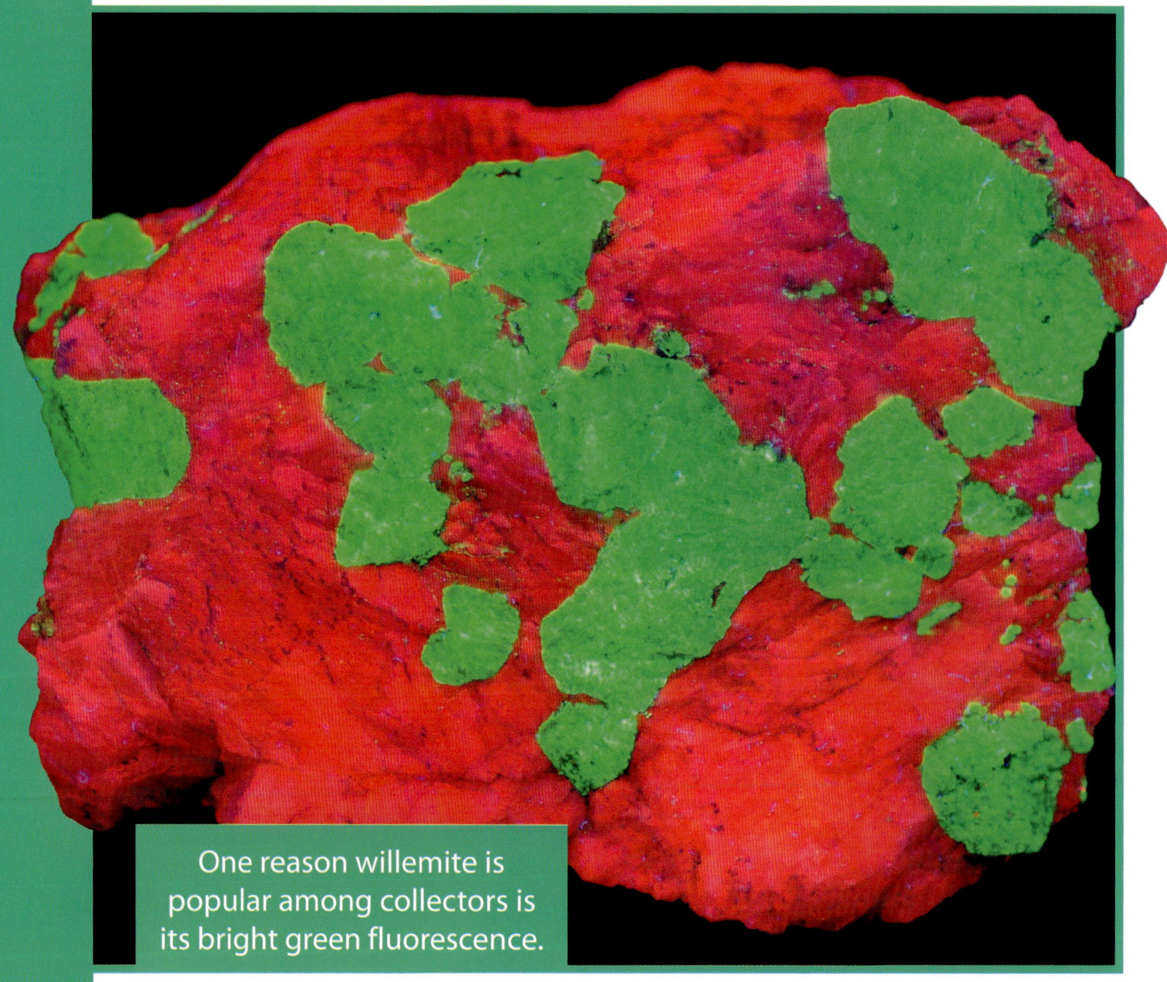

One reason willemite is popular among collectors is its bright green fluorescence.

Willemite has a hardness of only 5.5 on the Mohs scale. It is soft, fragile, and difficult to polish. For these reasons, it is not a good stone for jewelry.

ACROSS THE OCEAN

Willemite was first discovered in 1830 in Belgium. At the time, Belgium was part of the Netherlands. The gemstone was named after King William I of the Netherlands. The most famous willemite deposits are found in Franklin, New Jersey. The willemite from the Sterling Hill mine in this area is especially known for its glow.

WULFENITE

Wulfenite is a mineral that forms in sharp, rectangular crystals. Pure wulfenite is colorless. But most wulfenite displays shades from orangish red to yellowish orange. Wulfenite's bright coloring makes it easy to recognize. It is highly valued by collectors.

A COLLECTOR'S GEM

Wulfenite was first described in 1845. It was named after Austrian mineralogist Franz Xaver von Wulfen. Wulfenite can be found in many countries, including Namibia, Mexico, Morocco, and Slovenia.

Most wulfenite crystals are too thin and soft to be cut and used in jewelry. Wulfenite has a very low hardness rating on the Mohs scale. It measures 2.5 to 3. Instead, collectors seek it for its beauty and unique crystal shapes.

The Red Cloud Mine in Arizona is one of the most famous sources of wulfenite. It produces some of the deepest red wulfenite crystals in the world.

ZIRCON

Zircon is a gemstone that forms in many different types of rock. It may be white, yellow, orange, red, violet, blue, green, or black. The most popular and valuable zircon is colorless. These stones can sparkle with flashes of multicolored light, called fire. They are also known for their shine, or brilliance. Because of this, zircon looks very similar to diamond. Zircon is one of the birthstones for December.

Zircon is usually reddish brown.

CUTTING GEMS TO SHINE BRIGHT

Lapidaries shape gems with facets to help them shine. The three most basic styles are brilliant, step, and mixed. A brilliant cut has triangles and kite shapes that spread out from the middle. It sparkles more than any other shape. Step cuts shape the gem using long, flat rectangles. These look like steps going up to the top of the gem. Mixed cuts combine features of the two other cuts.

SHINING BRIGHTER

Starting in the 1920s, jewelers began heat-treating almost all zircon gemstones. This process can bring out brighter colors, such as blue and golden yellow. It can also make the stone colorless. Zircon has a hardness of 6 to 7.5 on the Mohs scale.

Most zircons are found as small pebbles in Thailand, Vietnam, Sri Lanka, and Cambodia. Zircon is also mined in other countries. These include Myanmar, Madagascar, Brazil, and Tanzania.

Zoisite is often found in a green-and-black pattern, showcasing both the crystals and the rock where they form.

ZOISITE

Zoisite is a crystal. When it is clear, colorful, or well formed, it is used as a gemstone. Zoisite forms in rocks that have gone through periods of high heat and pressure. It often grows when a mineral called plagioclase breaks down. Zoisite can form in many kinds of rocks. It sometimes grows as long crystals.

MIXED WITH RUBIES

Zoisite was discovered in the Saualpe Mountains in Austria in 1805. It was named after Austrian scholar Sigmund Zois, Baron von Edelstein. He provided money to fund mineral-collecting trips. In 1949, zoisite was discovered in Tanzania. A gem hunter named Tom Blevins found a large deposit of zoisite mixed with ruby crystals.

Today varieties of zoisite can be found in many countries. These include Tanzania, Kenya, Norway, Switzerland, Austria, India, Pakistan, and the United States. Zoisite ranges from 6 to 6.5 on the Mohs scale.

Jewelry is available showcasing both zoisite and ruby.

GLOSSARY

brittle
Easily broken, cracked, or shattered.

cavity
An unfilled space.

crust
In geology, the outer layer of Earth, which is made of rock and minerals.

element
A basic substance that cannot be broken down into anything simpler.

evaporate
To change from a liquid to a vapor or gas.

irritant
Something that causes discomfort.

mantle
The thick layer of melted rock between Earth's crust and its core.

metamorphic
Describing rocks that change in composition due to high heat and pressure underground.

microscopic
Visible only with a microscope.

mineral
A natural, inorganic solid substance made of one or more elements.

mollusk
A type of animal without a spine and with a shell.

molten
Turned into a liquid form due to heat.

organic
Related to living things.

prism
A three-dimensional shape with two identical, parallel faces connected by sides.

sedimentary
Describing rocks that form when layers of sediment, or minerals and organic matter carried by water, are compressed over time.

stalactite
A structure hanging from a cave ceiling, made of calcium salts deposited by dripping water.

trace element
A very small amount of an element in another substance.

transparent
See-through.

TO LEARN MORE

FURTHER READINGS

Berne, Emma Carlson. *Bling! 100 Fun Facts about Rocks and Gems.* National Geographic Kids, 2022.

Dennie, Devin. *An Anthology of Rocks and Minerals: A Collection of Rocks, Minerals, and Gems from Around the World*. DK, 2024.

Wheeler, Jill C. *The Mineral Encyclopedia*. Abdo, 2026.

ONLINE RESOURCES

To learn more about crystals and gemstones, please visit **abdobooklinks.com** or scan this QR code. These links are routinely monitored and updated to provide the most current information available.

INDEX

PHOTO CREDITS

Cover Photos: Dmytro Synelnychenko/Adobe Stock, front (agate); Shutterstock Images, front (amazonite, charoite, diamond, emerald, opal, sphene, sunstone); Sebastian Janicki/Shutterstock Images, front (amethyst); Serge Miles/Shutterstock Images, front (apatite); Minakryn Ruslan/Shutterstock Images, front (chrysocolla); Potapov Alexander/Shutterstock Images, front (citrine); Cagla Acikgoz/Shutterstock Images, front (rhodochrosite); Yut Chanthaburi/Shutterstock Images, front (sapphire); Subbotina Anna/Shutterstock Images, back (pearl); Albert Russ/Shutterstock Images, back (tanzanite); Asya Babushkina/Shutterstock Images, back (turquoise)

Interior Photos: Shutterstock Images, 1, 3 (top), 3 (bottom left), 3 (bottom right), 4 (left), 4 (right), 5, 7, 14–15, 17 (diamond), 21, 22–23, 24, 25, 26, 32–33, 37, 41, 44, 45, 46, 47 (top), 50, 51, 59, 60, 61, 62, 63, 64, 66, 67, 74, 75, 76, 77, 84, 85, 86, 87, 88, 88–89, 90, 92, 94, 96, 97, 98–99, 101, 102–103, 107, 108, 110–111, 111, 113, 114 (bottom), 121, 123, 125, 127, 128–129, 130, 132, 132–133, 135, 138, 139, 140, 141, 142, 143, 144, 145, 149, 150, 152, 152–153, 157, 159, 160, 161, 162, 164, 165, 168, 170, 171, 172, 173, 174, 175, 176–177, 179, 184, 185 (top), 185 (middle), 185 (bottom), 187; iStockphoto, 6, 20, 27, 30 (back), 38, 39, 52, 57, 147, 169; Minakryn Ruslan/Shutterstock Images, 8–9, 13, 17 (chrysocolla), 28, 35, 55, 72, 128, 134, 146, 182; Raka Firdaus/Shutterstock Images, 10; Red Line Editorial, 11; Yuriy Buyvol/Shutterstock Images, 12; Halyna Kubei/Alamy, 16, 79; Nick Knight/Shutterstock Images, 17 (alexandrite); Martin Stevko/Mindat.org, 17 (evenkite), 70–71; Albert Russ/Shutterstock Images, 17 (moldavite), 34, 69, 104, 105, 124, 183; DEA/A. Rizzi/De Agostini/Getty Images, 18; Anne Tipodees/Shutterstock Images, 19; Bjoern Wylezich/Shutterstock Images, 22, 56, 80 (top), 154; Corbin17/Alamy, 29, 100; The Natural History Museum, London/Science Source, 30 (front), 166–167, 167; Roy Palmer/Shutterstock Images, 31; Serge Miles/Shutterstock Images, 32; Marli Miller/UCG/Universal Images Group/Getty Images, 36–37; Andriy Kananovych/Shutterstock Images, 40, 155; DK Images/Science Source, 42; Luca Lorenzelli/Shutterstock Images, 43; Potapov Alexander/Shutterstock Images, 47 (bottom); Weng Xinyang/Xinhua News Agency/Getty Images, 48, 49; Ono Bawono/Shutterstock Images, 53; Cagla Acikgoz/Shutterstock Images, 54, 65, 136, 156–157, 176; Sebastian Janicki/Shutterstock Images, 58; Harry Taylor/Dorling Kindersley/Science Source, 68; Kimberly Boyles/Shutterstock Images, 72–73; Dan Olsen/Shutterstock Images, 78; Peter Hermes Furian/Shutterstock Images, 80 (bottom); Olga Anourina/Shutterstock Images, 81; TommyK/Alamy, 82; Ioana Bica/Shutterstock Images, 83; Ron Evans/Alamy, 91; PB/YB/Alamy, 93; Yuko Ishizawa/Shutterstock Images, 95; Marina Kryuchina/Shutterstock Images, 99; Svetlana Beleacov/Shutterstock Images, 102; Jimena Terraza/Shutterstock Images, 106; DEA/Photo 1/De Agostini/Getty Images, 109; Viktoria Prusakova/Shutterstock Images, 112; PjrRocks/Alamy, 114 (top); José María Barres Manuel/Alamy, 115; Robert M. Lavinsky/Mindat.org, 116; Han Myo Htun/Shutterstock Images, 116–117; Dem Bautz/Shutterstock Images, 118; Robert Hradil/Getty Images for Sotheby's/Getty Images Entertainment/Getty Images, 119, 158; Subbotina Anna/Shutterstock Images, 120; David G. Hayes/Shutterstock Images, 122; SBS Eclectic Images/Alamy, 126; Andriana Syvanych/Shutterstock Images, 131; Lyn Alweis/Denver Post/Getty Images, 137; Mike Greenslade/VW Pics/Science Source, 148; Science Stock Photography/Science Source, 151; Aleksei Kochev/Shutterstock Images, 163; Asya Babushkina/Shutterstock Images, 178; Breck P. Kent/Shutterstock Images, 180; De Agostini Picture Library/Getty Images, 181; Moha El-Jaw/Shutterstock Images, 186

ABDOBOOKS.COM

Published by Abdo Reference, a division of ABDO, PO Box 398166, Minneapolis, Minnesota 55439. Copyright © 2026 by Abdo Consulting Group, Inc. International copyrights reserved in all countries. No part of this book may be reproduced in any form without written permission from the publisher. Encyclopedias™ is a trademark and logo of Abdo Reference.

Printed in China.
082025
012026

Editor: Marley Richmond
Series Designer: Colleen McLaren
Production Designer: Ebonee Estrella

LIBRARY OF CONGRESS CONTROL NUMBER: 2025939304

PUBLISHER'S CATALOGING-IN-PUBLICATION DATA

Names: Bell, Samantha S., author.
Title: The crystal and gemstone encyclopedia / by Samantha S. Bell
Description: Minneapolis, Minnesota: Abdo Reference, 2026 | Series: Geology encyclopedias | Includes online resources and index.
Identifiers: ISBN 9781098298883 (lib. bdg.) | ISBN 9798384932680 (ebook)
Subjects: LCSH: Crystals--Juvenile literature. | Precious stones--Juvenile literature. | Rocks--Juvenile literature. | Geology--Juvenile literature. | Encyclopedias--Juvenile literature.
Classification: DDC 553.8--dc23